Equity, Diversity & Inclusion

In Hong Kong

A quantitative approach and in-depth analysis

Bryan Law

Fox College of Business

First edition: June 2022

Revised edition: September 2022

Fox College of Business

Disclaimer

Fox College of Business and Bryan Law are not engaged in rendering legal, accounting, real estate, or other professional services. This book should not be relied upon as providing such advice. We strongly urge that you seek professional advice prior to acting on the information contained herein.

The information contained herein has been obtained from sources that we believe are reliable, but we cannot guarantee its accuracy or completeness. Fox College of Business, Bryan Law, and every person involved in creating this book disclaim any warranty as to the accuracy, completeness, and currency of the contents of this book. We also disclaim all liability in respect of the results of any action taken or not taken in reliance upon information in this book.

Bryan Law B.Math., LL.M., LL.D.

Bryan is an entrepreneur with a diversified professional background. He has over 25 years of experience in strategy, analysis, franchise, education, training and development. Besides being a management consultant, Bryan is a legal researcher in various areas, including discrimination, contract, environmental, human rights, labour, privacy, and real estate law.

He was a certified instructor, professor, and legal and real estate subject matter expert at various business colleges and education providers. He provided one-on-one training to the management levels in corporations, including C-level executives in public companies.

He authored over 40 books on various topics, including real estate, human resources, creative thinking, entrepreneurship and human rights. Bryan's wide-ranging knowledge and professional experience, coupled with excellent training and coaching skills, have placed him as one of the foremost management consultants and trainers in Canada.

Table of Contents

1. Introduction

ESG

ESG is the acronym for Environmental, Social and Governance. It is used to reflect an organization's corporate financial interests that focus mainly on sustainability and ethical impacts. Since prudent investors only invest their capital in corporations that would have long-term solid performance, they use ESG criteria as the indicator of sustainability. More and more countries require listed companies to file ESG reports annually, which has become a norm.

Environmental

For environmental criteria, it is a corporate responsibility to the public. The main objectives are to avoid contamination, reduce pollution and preserve the environment through internal and external methods. Manufacturers will prevent contaminants, such as not using chlorine as the bleaching agent and reducing the use of heavy metals. Companies will use recyclable or decomposable materials to replace plastics, especially single-use utensils in fast food restaurants.

Another objective is to reduce carbon footprint. Common methods include purchasing parts and products from local manufacturers to reduce the carbon dioxide produced by transportation and using green energy such as wind and solar power. Trees are crucial assets to protect the environment. Some corporations offer to plant one tree for each product they sell, such as T-shirts. That kind of promotion effectively preserves the environment and enhances the corporate image.

While corporations can contribute to environmental protection internally by using energy-saving equipment, environmentally friendly materials and products, they can also achieve the same goal by outside forces. For example, corporations can rent their offices in green buildings and buy supplies from green suppliers.

Social

Corporations have social responsibilities to the public and their employees. The fundamental duty is to comply with human rights law. Most Western countries have consolidated legislation to protect human rights, but not Hong Kong. Instead, Hong Kong has four ordinances to protect people from disability, family status, race and sex discrimination. The Equal Opportunities Commission is responsible for enforcing those ordinances.

All corporations must ensure that they provide customers with non-discriminatory access to their services and employees with non-discriminatory HR policies. For example, they should offer ramps for wheelchairs access to their workplaces, facilities and stores.

EDI is an essential part of ESG, forming an independent study branch. It is the acronym for Equity, Diversity and Inclusion. Corporations should fairly treat customers, suppliers and employees with an inclusive culture. Corporations can benefit from a diverse workforce and customer base, and some extend their diversity policy to suppliers, too.

Most investors will only invest in companies that produce responsible products. They will not invest in companies that manufacture tobacco, firearms and alcohol products. Data privacy, product quality and safety are also factors to be considered when investors consider choosing companies to invest in.

One of the social responsibilities is to protect the health and safety of customers and employees. The products produced, venue and equipment provided should be safe and healthy. Besides physical health, the mental health of employees is also vital to corporations. Emphasizing the importance of a work-life balance has become the norm in corporate cultures.

Governance

In governance, investors will examine the compliance, business ethics, management quality, board independence and shareholder democracy of the company that interests them.

All corporations must file their tax returns annually, which is part of compliance. Listed companies must file their financial statements quarterly and annually, along with other disclosures and reports such as management discussion and analysis. ESG reporting may also be required.

Some industries, such as banks, law firms and industrial companies, will also have their regulatory compliance. For example, there are many compliance procedures for banks to protect their customers, and law firms must set up and reconcile their trust accounts. Industrial companies must comply with environmental laws to use and store chemicals.

The business ethics of a company is essential. Some corporations may be members of a business association, such as the Better Business Bureau in North America, and they have a set of business conducts to follow. If it is a regulated business, the corporation must also follow the professional code of ethics. Investors will also study the online rating of the company before investing.

The quality of the management team is crucial. Investors want the team to be a well-rounded one. For example, the founders of a tech company usually come from the technical field. However, the management team needs other expertise in finance, HR, general management, sales and marketing. Investors also want to know about the management style, philosophy and mission statement. Some companies may show their political or cultural attitudes, which will affect the investors' decisions.

For board independence, the directors should not be the employees of the company to avoid any conflict of interest. Also, they should not be a relative of an executive of the company. All directors should preferably have no affiliation with any government agency or lobbying agent to avoid biased decisions and conflicts.

Since the investors will become shareholders, shareholder democracy is an important issue. They want to ensure access to information, have voting rights on major issues, have a say in executive compensation, and have more say in director elections.

EDI

More and more corporations, organizations and governments promote equity, diversity and inclusion as their core values. The propelling force behind that is not only because of justice — to eliminate the systemic discrimination that identifiable groups, such as women, older adults and visible minorities, have experienced by increasing their representation in employment, education and other opportunities. An equitable, diverse, and inclusive environment can also promote those organizations' images and reputations and enable their employees, contractors, and business partners to reach their full potential and contribute their best by feeling respected, treated fairly, and working in comfortable environments.

Equity is the fair and respectful treatment of all people, especially those working for the organization. With an appropriate approach to carrying out equity, people can eventually get equality in the workplace and in society. However, that is not an easy task. The critical point of the issue is how to treat people fairly and respectfully.

Take the COVID-19 vaccination as an example. Some countries require people to show proof of COVID-19 vaccination to travel[1] or access certain businesses and settings.[2] Such evidence is often stored in a cell phone app with a tracing function to locate that person for preventive measures. Some people may not be able to afford a smartphone or data plan and thus may not be able to cope with the new rule. [3] That creates unfairness to those underrepresented groups.

The vaccination rates in the United States varied among different ethnic groups. The percentage of white and

---

[1] "'Vaccine passports' are on the way, but developing them won't be easy", Washington Post, last updated March 28, 2021, https://www.washingtonpost.com/health/2021/03/28/vaccine-passports-for-work/
[2] "Proof of COVID-19 vaccination", Government of Ontario, last accessed October 24, 2021, https://covid-19.ontario.ca/proof-covid-19-vaccination
[3] "Hong Kong's 'Leave Home Safe' mandate amounts to differential treatment, equality watchdog chief warns", South China Morning Post, last updated October 23, 2021, https://www.scmp.com/news/hong-kong/politics/article/3153460/hong-kongs-leave-home-safe-mandate-amounts-differential

Asia Americans who had received at least one dose of the COVID-19 vaccine was significantly higher than that of Indigenous, Hispanic and black Americans.[4] Such disparities were due to non-inclusive policies, such as the poor selection of vaccination sites, which increased the transportation costs and time that are unaffordable at the grassroots level; the majority are blacks and Hispanics. In addition, most of the vaccination appointment time was during working hours, and most working-class people could not take time off to get vaccinated during working hours.[5] As a result, the people in the US did not have equal access to vaccination due to their income class or wealth level.

Similarly, the global vaccination rates among countries also reflected inequality between developed and developing countries. Western countries are high-income countries, and they were alleged that they had hoarded Covid-19 vaccines much more than they needed.[6] The low-income countries, mainly Latin America and Africa, did not get enough vaccines for their people. The countries in Africa were left behind with the lowest vaccination rates. Most of them had less than a 1%

---

[4] "Inoculation Nation: Available Covid-19 Vaccine Data Shows Uneven Access By Race And Ethnicity", American Public Media, last updated May 21, 2021, https://www.apmresearchlab.org/covid/vaccines-by-race

[5] "Why Black And Latino People Still Lag On COVID Vaccines — And How To Fix It", National Public Radio, last updated April 26, 2021, https://www.npr.org/sections/health-shots/2021/04/26/989962041/why-black-and-latino-people-still-lag-on-covid-vaccines-and-how-to-fix-it

[6] "Western countries have 'hoarded' Covid vaccines. Africa is being left behind as cases surge", The Cable News Network, last updated February 5, 2021, https://www.cnn.com/2021/02/05/africa/vaccine-race-africa-intl/index.html

fully vaccinated rate as of July 6, 2021, [7] more than six months after the first vaccine was produced.[8] Even with the help of the United Nations, vaccine equity was still challenging. The UN reported that 82% of the vaccines had gone to high or upper-middle-income countries, while only 0.2% had been sent to low-income countries.[9]

Such dramatic inequity in vaccine coverage in the US and the world shows that equity and diversity serve not only different ethnicities, sex, age or religious groups but also groups with varying income levels.

Diversity deals with demographic issues, focusing on the equal representation of disadvantaged groups. Every country, city or community has its demographic mix. People have different education levels, are of different ages, belong to another gender, believe in different religions, and belong to other ethnic groups.

Since people come from different groups with different backgrounds, we must provide an environment where everyone feels welcome, is treated with respect, and can participate in activities fully without worrying about being

---

[7] "Tracking Coronavirus Vaccinations Around the World", New York Times, last updated July 6, 2021, https://www.nytimes.com/interactive/2021/world/covid-vaccinations-tracker.html

[8] "COVID-19 vaccine", Wikipedia, last accessed September 23, 2023, https://en.wikipedia.org/wiki/COVID-19_vaccine

[9] "Vaccine equity the 'challenge of our time', WHO chief declares, as governments call for solidarity, sharing", The United Nations, last updated April 16, 2021, https://news.un.org/en/story/2021/04/1089972

isolated. Inclusion can do that, but we must achieve diversity before giving those people a comfortable and fair environment.

Many people, however, still stay at the surface level when dealing with equity, diversity and inclusion. They also think that equity and diversity are absolute. For example, the employee per ethnic ratio should be based on the population of society. Say, if there are only two ethnic groups, A and B, in the society and the ratio of the two groups is 7:3, then the corporations should employ people of the two ethnic groups in the ratio of 7:3, too. That is, 70% of their employees should be from ethnic group A, and 30% of them should be from B.

Similarly, they believe that if a country has 50% of people belonging to ethnic A, 40% of people belonging to ethnic B, 9% of people belonging to ethnic C, and 1% of people belonging to ethnic D, a corporation in that country should hire people according to that ratio to show diversity as well. That type of equity is absolute in nature but may not achieve true equity.

While equity should not be absolutely based on a ratio, it is not limited to ethnic issues. Similarly, diversity also includes people of different natures rather than being restricted to people of other races. Basically, all the grounds related to human rights, including age, ancestry, colour, citizenship, creed, disability, ethnic origin, family status, marital status, place of origin, race, the record of offences, sex, and sexual orientation, should be considered in diversity.

Therefore, diversity cannot rely on a single set of data, and employment rates should not be strictly proportional to the ethnic populations or a single trait.

The concept of EDI should be generic and have the same value in all countries, although demographics are not the same and will affect the Points System discussed in Chapter 7. The Canadian cases should also be considered when applying the principles in Hong Kong, especially when Hong Kong lacks such precedents.

2. Historical Disadvantages

All types of discrimination are rooted in historical and contemporary injustices and prejudices. Discrimination puts different groups of people in disadvantaged positions, and they are mistreated at work and in society. Sexism, ageism, and racism are the oldest and most common misconceptions that eventually turned into discrimination. Two other types of discrimination with a long history are discrimination against persons with disabilities and people with different creeds.

Sexism

Sexual discrimination has the most extended history of all types of discrimination because two different genders have lived together since the existence of human beings. That was due to the physical differences between males and females and the preferences of females who wanted to do different jobs. The physical differences between the two genders made people believe that females were the weaker ones. However, we cannot say males are more capable than females or vice versa. It depends on the nature of the jobs.

An old saying in ancient China, "*Women's ignorance is a virtue.*"[10] That is an embodiment of male chauvinism. Fortunately, Mao Zedong[11] put forward the slogan "*Women hold up half the sky*" in 1955,[12] which significantly changed the status of women in China. China implemented the policy of equal pay for men and women for equal work about ten years earlier than the United States.[13]

In the modern Western world, women have also been treated unjustly. The United Kingdom and Canada did not treat women as "persons". The British North America (BNA) Act,[14] passed by the British Parliament in 1867 to create the Dominion of Canada, did not address any issue of basic women's rights. Therefore, the Supreme Court of Canada in 1928 ruled that women were not "persons" according to the BNA Act. As a result, women in Canada were ineligible for appointments to the Senate. The Famous Five[15] appealed to the Judicial Committee of the Privy Council in Britain in 1929,

[10] "Ancient China's 'Virtuous' Women", The World of Chinese, last updated October 20, 2015, https://www.theworldofchinese.com/2015/10/ancient-chinas-virtuous-women/

[11] "Mao Zedong", Wikipedia, last accessed September 23, 2023, https://en.wikipedia.org/wiki/Mao_Zedong

[12] "Women hold up half the sky poster work on paper", Oakland Museum of California, last accessed September 23, 2023, http://collections.museumca.org/?q=collection-item/2010541020

[13] "The Equal Pay Act of 1963", Government of the United States, last accessed September 23, 2023, https://www.eeoc.gov/statutes/equal-pay-act-1963

[14] "Constitution Act, 1867", The Canadian Encyclopedia, last updated April 24, 2020, https://thecanadianencyclopedia.ca/en/article/constitution-act-1867

[15] "Famous Five", The Canadian Encyclopedia, last updated June 4, 2015, https://www.thecanadianencyclopedia.ca/en/article/famous-5

and the British Privy Council then decided that women were, in fact, "persons" under the BNA Act.[16]

In *Chapdelaine v. Air Canada*,[17] a group of females possessed all of the qualifications necessary to be a pilot when they applied for the position but were rejected by the airline because they failed to meet the minimum height requirement of five feet and six inches. Such condition based on their height was ruled as discrimination under the human rights code, as it was a discriminatory practice on the ground of sex. The human rights tribunal reasoned that over 82% of females in Canada between 20 and 29 years of age were shorter than five feet and six inches at the time, while only 11% of men in the same age category were shorter than that height. Therefore, such a minimum height policy would disqualify 82% of all such women but only 11% of all men from becoming pilots, putting women in an unfairly disadvantaged position.

Sexism also exists in other industries, such as the technology field. A Google engineer sent out an anti-diversity manifesto[18] and was fired.[19]

[16] "Persons Case", The Canadian Encyclopedia, last updated October 18, 2019, https://www.thecanadianencyclopedia.ca/en/article/persons-case
[17] 1987 CanLII 102 (CHRT)
[18] "Google Employee's Anti-Diversity Manifesto on Women's 'Neuroticism' Goes Viral", NBC Universal, last update August 7, 2017, https://www.nbcnews.com/business/business-news/google-employee-s-anti-diversity-manifesto-women-s-neuroticism-goes-n790401
[19] "James Damore, Google engineer fired for writing manifesto on women's 'neuroticism,' sues company", NBC Universal, last update January 18, 2018, https://www.nbcnews.com/news/us-news/google-

Women's participation in many areas remains low as men still dominate them and are reluctant to make changes. For example, although reports indicate female fighter pilots are more careful and excel in certain tasks, such as operating delicate equipment,[20] many countries still have female fighter pilots.[21] Even for commercial pilots, the situation is the same. As of December 2019, only 5.4% of all certified civilian pilots in the United States were women and about 3% worldwide.[22]

Other than the resistance from the male-dominated environment, there is another reason why women's participation in certain fields is low. Like men, most women pick their study subjects and occupations by personal interests, not their abilities. Many female students with excellent academic performance did not choose engineering, medicine, or science subjects as their major studies, not because they could not enter those disciplines but because their interests were in other areas. That leads, unfortunately, to fewer female engineers, medical doctors and scientists. As a result, people mistakenly think males perform better than females in those areas and start labelling that females are incapable of studying or doing those jobs.

engineer-fired-writing-manifesto-women-s-neuroticism-sues-company-n835836

[20] "Female pilots endure hardship to serve in China's air force", Global Times, last updated November 13, 2016, https://www.globaltimes.cn/content/1017639.shtml

[21] "Fighter pilot", Wikipedia, last accessed September 23, 2023, https://en.wikipedia.org/wiki/Fighter_pilot

[22] "Women in aviation", Wikipedia, last accessed September 23, 2023, https://en.wikipedia.org/wiki/Women_in_aviation

Ageism

Just like women, older adults were considered weak because they lacked the power to hunt animals. Since the age of troglodytes, they have been discriminated against, and age discrimination occurs daily in today's society.[23] Stereotypes about older workers are also widespread in our society. Older workers are often unfairly perceived as less committed to their jobs, not energetic, not creative, less productive, unreceptive to change, and unable or costly to be trained. A survey shows that over 80% of Canadians interviewed say ageism exists in hiring.[24]

When some employers publish job advertisements, they often inadvertently express age restrictions, norms or preferences. For example, an employment advertisement that says, *"The company is looking for a young and energetic person,"* shows an age preference. That is discrimination against older people, so it should not be used or allowed to be used.

Most governments have legislation to protect citizens from age discrimination, especially in employment. For

---

[23] "5 Examples of Everyday Ageism", South Dakota State University, last updated February 21, 2020, https://extension.sdstate.edu/5-examples-everyday-ageism

[24] "8 Out Of 10 Say Ageism Exists in Hiring", GlobeNewswire, last updated February 12, 2020, https://www.globenewswire.com/news-release/2020/02/12/1983924/0/en/8-Out-Of-10-Say-Ageism-Exists-in-Hiring.html

example, the Age Discrimination in Employment Act (ADEA) in the United States prohibits age discrimination against people aged 40 or older.[25] However, people younger than 40 are not protected under that law.

Mandatory retirement may be a kind of discrimination as it forces older adults to quit their jobs. Many jurisdictions allow mandatory retirement at a certain age, say 65. The question is: Why must people be mandatorily retired at 65 when the general health conditions of people in our society are improving? Setting the retirement age at a certain age has been reviewed by some governments. Some of them ruled that mandatory retirement age is discriminative,[26] but some still allow such practice and say it is supported by the human rights code.[27]

In Canada, its Supreme Court ruled that employers should be allowed to discriminate on the basis of age when there is a reasonable and bona fide qualification because of the nature of the employment. The court set out two tests to determine whether a mandatory retirement scheme is justifiable:

---

[25] "Age Discrimination", U.S. Equal Employment Opportunity Commission, last accessed September 23, 2023, https://www.eeoc.gov/age-discrimination

[26] *McKinney v. University of Guelph*, 1990 CanLII 60 (SCC), [1990] 3 SCR 229

[27] *Dickason v. University of Alberta*, 1992 CanLII 30 (SCC), [1992] 2 SCR 1103

1. *It must be imposed honestly, in good faith, and in the belief that such limitation is imposed in the interests of the adequate performance of the work involved with all reasonable dispatch, safety and economy, and not for ulterior or extraneous reasons aimed at objectives which could defeat the purpose of the Code.*

2. *It must be related in an objective sense to the performance of the employment concerned, in that it is reasonably necessary to assure the efficient and economical performance of the job without endangering the employee, his fellow employees and the general public.*[28]

There is also considerable evidence of discrimination against older adults in the healthcare system[29], which is a growing concern.[30] For example, a 71-year-old Canadian man who was legally blind applied to the provincial Assistive Devices Program for financial assistance in purchasing a closed-circuit television magnifier. The device would enable him to read and do other tasks involving fine visual acuity. His application was denied as there was an age limit (up to 18 at

---

[28] *Ontario Human Rights Commission v. Etobicoke*, 1982 CanLII 15 (SCC), [1982] 1 SCR 202

[29] "NHS accused of age discrimination over lifesaving surgery", The Guardian, last updated October 15, 2012, https://www.theguardian.com/society/2012/oct/15/nhs-cancer-joints-surgery-age-discrimination

[30] "Why Ageism in Health Care Is a Growing Concern", Regis College, last accessed May 26, 2021, https://online.regiscollege.edu/blog/why-ageism-in-health-care-is-a-growing-concern/

that time) for funding the visual aids. The Court of Appeal ruled that such practice is discriminatory. [31]

A recent report released by the United Nations also shows that about half of the population in the world has ageist attitudes. It leads to poor physical and mental health and reduced quality of life for older persons.[32]

Racism

Since discovering the new world,[33] almost all Western countries have had discrimination issues concerning Indigenous peoples, especially the Americas and Oceania. There are over 250 million Indigenous people worldwide,[34] and they face eviction from their ancestral lands, being denied the opportunity to equal access to services, education, employment and justice. Indigenous people are often marginalized and face discrimination in countries' legal systems. They may not express their culture and may be treated discriminatorily and even under physical attacks. Most

---

[31] *Ontario (Human Rights Commission) v. Ontario*, 1994 CanLII 1590 (ON CA)

[32] "Ageism leads to poorer health, social isolation, earlier deaths and cost economies billions: report calls for swift action to implement effective anti-ageism strategies", World Health Organization, last updated March 18, 2021, https://www.who.int/news/item/18-03-2021-ageism-is-a-global-challenge-un

[33] "New World", Wikipedia, last accessed September 23, 2023, https://en.wikipedia.org/wiki/New_World

[34] "Indigenous peoples", Wikipedia, last accessed September 23, 2023, https://en.wikipedia.org/wiki/Indigenous_peoples

countries have legislation to protect Indigenous people and assist them in housing, education and other areas.

The United Nations General Assembly adopted the United Nations Declaration on the Rights of Indigenous Peoples (UNDRIP) in 2007. UNDRIP addresses individual and collective rights, cultural rights and identity, and rights to education, health, employment, language, and others. It protects Indigenous peoples' rights, including on issues relating to land, culture, identity, religion, language, health, education, governance and community. A majority of 144 states voted to favour it, and four voted against it. The four countries that voted against it were Australia, Canada, New Zealand, and the United States.[35] Although those four countries later also endorsed the principles of UNDRIP, their votes in the United Nations told the world how they would treat the Indigenous people.

Since the genocide of Indigenous people, the Americans' discrimination and suppression of other ethnic groups have shown no sign of stopping.[36] Incidents of racial discrimination in the United States can be said to be endless.[37] Because society discriminates against Blacks

---

[35] "United Nations Declaration on the Rights of Indigenous Peoples", United Nations, last accessed September 23, 2023, https://www.un.org/development/desa/indigenouspeoples/declaration-on-the-rights-of-indigenous-peoples.html

[36] "United States war crimes", Wikipedia, last accessed September 23, 2023, https://en.wikipedia.org/wiki/United_States_war_crimes

[37] "Discrimination in the United States", Wikipedia, last accessed September 23, 2023, https://en.wikipedia.org/wiki/Discrimination_in_the_United_States

systematically and law enforcement agencies continue to have violence against Blacks, on and off, there are social movements in protest against police brutality incidents and all racially motivated violence against Black people. The recent Black Lives Matter has spread to almost every Western country.[38]

Although a well-known statement on human rights was written in the second paragraph of the United States Declaration of Independence,[39] which stated that *"all men are created equal"*,[40] that concept established in 1776 did not apply to non-white people. Slavery was still allowed until Abraham Lincoln[41] abolished it in 1865. Today, human rights in the United States are still not protected well enough, which invites criticism.

For example, golf is one of the most popular single sports in the United States.[42] Although three out of the four

---

[38] "Black Lives Matter", Wikipedia, last accessed September 23, 2023, https://en.wikipedia.org/wiki/Black_Lives_Matter

[39] "United States Declaration of Independence", Wikipedia, last accessed September 23, 2023, https://en.wikipedia.org/wiki/United_States_Declaration_of_Independence

[40] "All men are created equal", Wikipedia, last accessed September 23, 2023, https://en.wikipedia.org/wiki/All_men_are_created_equal

[41] "Thirteenth Amendment to the United States Constitution", Wikipedia, last accessed September 23, 2023, https://en.wikipedia.org/wiki/Thirteenth_Amendment_to_the_United_States_Constitution

[42] "Sports in the United States", Wikipedia, last accessed September 23, 2023, https://en.wikipedia.org/wiki/Sports_in_the_United_States

major international golf championships[43] are held in the United States, the golf industry in the United States is full of sexism and racial discrimination.

Since its opening in 1977, the famous Shoal Creek Club[44] has never had a female member until 2009. It only accepted two female members in 2009, and they are the only two female members so far. Another equally famous Augusta Golf Club opened in 1934 and did not accept female members until 2012. Coincidentally, among the four female members of the two golf clubs, one of them is repeated and is the former Secretary of State Condoleezza Rice.[45] Another famous club, Cypress Points Club,[46] still does not accept Black people as members for more than 90 years. Allowing such practices encourages sexism and racial discrimination in disguise.

Like the United States, the United Kingdom has a history of enslaving Africans.[47] Although legislation such as the Human Rights Act 1998[48] and the Race Relations

---

[43] "Men's major golf championships", Wikipedia, last accessed September 23, 2023,
https://en.wikipedia.org/wiki/Men%27s_major_golf_championships

[44] "Shoal Creek Club", Wikipedia, last accessed September 23, 2023,
https://en.wikipedia.org/wiki/Shoal_Creek_Club

[45] "Condoleezza Rice", Wikipedia, last accessed September 23, 2023,
https://en.wikipedia.org/wiki/Condoleezza_Rice

[46] "Cypress Point Club", Wikipedia, last accessed September 23, 2023,
https://en.wikipedia.org/wiki/Cypress_Point_Club

[47] "Slavery in Britain", Wikipedia, last accessed September 23, 2023,
https://en.wikipedia.org/wiki/Slavery_in_Britain

[48] "Human Rights Act 1998", Government of the United Kingdom, last accessed September 23, 2023,
https://www.legislation.gov.uk/ukpga/1998/42/contents

(Amendment) Act[49] promotes and protects racial equality, and UK Prime Minister Johnson said that the United Kingdom is not a racist country, many Black Britons disagree.[50] According to a 2014 British Social Attitudes survey,[51] one-third of Britons admit to being racially prejudiced.[52] The most recent incident is that after England had lost its 2020 Euro Cup, racist abuse targeted three black English players who missed the penalty kicks.[53]

India is the biggest democratic country in the world, but it has a severe problem of racial discrimination. Historically, India's caste system[54] divided its people into four classes:[55]

[49] "Race Relations (Amendment) Act 2000", Government of the United Kingdom, last accessed September 23, 2023, https://www.legislation.gov.uk/ukpga/2000/34/contents

[50] "Boris Johnson says the UK isn't a racist country. Black Britons disagree", The Independent, last updated June 9, 2020, https://www.independent.co.uk/life-style/boris-johnson-racism-uk-george-floyd-protests-black-lives-matter-a9556756.html

[51] "British Social Attitudes 36", NatCen Social Research, last accessed September 23, 2023, https://www.natcen.ac.uk/our-research/research/british-social-attitudes/

[52] "One third of Britons 'admit being racially prejudiced'", The British Broadcasting Corporation, last updated May 28, 2014, https://www.bbc.com/news/uk-27599401

[53] "Black players targets of racist attacks after England's Euro Cup loss", The Canadian Broadcasting Corporation, last updated July 12, 2021, https://www.cbc.ca/player/play/1920833091919

[54] "Caste system in India", Wikipedia, last accessed September 23, 2023, https://en.wikipedia.org/wiki/Caste_system_in_India

[55] "What is India's caste system?", The British Broadcasting Corporation, last updated June 19, 2019, https://www.bbc.com/news/world-asia-india-35650616

Brahmin,[56] Kshatriya,[57] Vaishya,[58] and Shudra.[59] Brahmins specialized as priests and teachers and were the head of the hierarchy. Kshatriyas were warriors and rulers and were ranked second in the caste system. The third rank was Vaishyas; they were farmers, traders and merchants. Shudras had the lowest status among the four, and they were peasants and labourers.

With the development of society, various castes branched into many levels. In addition to the four major castes, another type of people, called Dalit[60] or untouchable, is excluded from the castes. They have the lowest social status and are most discriminated against by society. Most of them are street sweepers, latrine cleaners and coolies.

Although Article 15 of the Constitution of India stipulates that *The State shall not discriminate against any citizen on grounds only of religion, race, caste, sex, place of birth or any of them*[61] , and Article 17 also states *"Untouchability" is abolished and its practice in any form is*

[56] "Brahmin", Wikipedia, last accessed September 23, 2023, https://en.wikipedia.org/wiki/Brahmin
[57] "Kshatriya", Wikipedia, last accessed September 23, 2023, https://en.wikipedia.org/wiki/Kshatriya
[58] "Vaishya", Wikipedia, last accessed September 23, 2023, https://en.wikipedia.org/wiki/Vaishya
[59] "Shudra", Wikipedia, last accessed September 23, 2023, https://en.wikipedia.org/wiki/Shudra
[60] "Dalit", Wikipedia, last accessed September 23, 2023 https://en.wikipedia.org/wiki/Dalit
[61] "The Constitution of India", Government of India, last accessed September 23, 2023, https://www.india.gov.in/sites/upload_files/npi/files/coi_part_full.pdf

forbidden,[62] discrimination based on the caste system is still a common problem in India.

The punishment of refusal to recognize the caste relationship may cause serious consequences, such as being publicly lynched to death by family members. Marriages between different castes may also lead to large-scale attacks on lower-caste communities.[63]

The caste is hereditary. The caste system has profoundly impacted millions of people's daily lives and customs for thousands of years. Racial discrimination has not been eliminated, especially in the vast rural areas. Similar caste systems also exist in Nepal and Sri Lanka.[64] Even in the US and the most 'civilized' cyber industry in Silicon Valley, the caste system still affects Indian workers[65].

Although many developed countries have legislation to fight racism, the problem is ongoing. For example, the Constitution of France[66] states that *It shall ensure the equality of all citizens before the law, without distinction of origin, race*

[62] Ditto
[63] "Caste Discrimination: A Global Concern", Human Rights Watch for the United Nations, last accessed September 23, 2023, https://www.hrw.org/reports/2001/globalcaste/caste0801-03.htm
[64] Ditto
[65] "India's engineers have thrived in Silicon Valley. So has its caste system.", Washington Post, last updated Oct. 27, 2020, https://www.washingtonpost.com/technology/2020/10/27/indian-caste-bias-silicon-valley/
[66] "France's Constitution of 1958 with Amendments through 2008", Constitute, last accessed September 23, 2023, https://www.constituteproject.org/constitution/France_2008.pdf

or religion; racism is still regarded by many as an important social issue in French society. Racism against Jews has a long history in France, and other targets include Algerians, Berbers and Arabs.[67]

Racism in France is still a hot issue. The French National Human Rights Commission reported in 2016 that 8% of French people believe that certain races are superior to others.[68] It is believed that the terrorist attacks in France in 2015[69] led to an increase in the number of people with Islamophobia,[70] and the solid social opposition to Muslims increased the number of racist acts. According to a French National Human Rights Commission survey, 34% of the French population has a negative attitude towards Islam. Half of them believe that Islam is a menace to their national identity. Besides, 41% believe Jews have a singular relationship with money, while 20% believe Jews have too much power in France.

Racial discrimination exists all over the world, including in communist countries such as Vietnam. The international society has accused the Vietnamese government of

[67] "Racism in France", Wikipedia, last accessed September 23, 2023, https://en.wikipedia.org/wiki/Racism_in_France
[68] Ditto
[69] "November 2015 Paris attacks", Wikipedia, last accessed September 23, 2023, https://en.wikipedia.org/wiki/November_2015_Paris_attacks
[70] "Islamophobia", Wikipedia, last accessed September 23, 2023, https://en.wikipedia.org/wiki/Islamophobia

discriminating[71] against the Chams,[72] the Vietnamese Montagnard,[73] and the Khmer Krom.[74]

Creed

All people should be treated the same way, have access to the same opportunities and benefits, and be dealt with equal dignity and respect, regardless of their creed. Creed is not a well-defined term, but the courts and tribunals have often referred to religious beliefs and practices. In some jurisdictions, such as the Government of Canada, the term *religion* is used instead of *creed*. However, several decisions[75] have recognized that the term 'creed' can mean more than religion.

In Canada, the court ruled that when a rule or policy conflicts with religious practice, the organization must ensure that the affected individuals can observe their religion unless this would cause undue hardship because of cost or health and safety reasons. According to the Ontario Human Rights

---

[71] "Racism in Vietnam", Wikipedia, last accessed September 23, 2023, https://en.wikipedia.org/wiki/Racism_in_Vietnam

[72] "Chams", Wikipedia, last accessed September 23, 2023, https://en.wikipedia.org/wiki/Chams

[73] "Montagnard (Vietnam)", Wikipedia, last accessed September 23, 2023, https://en.wikipedia.org/wiki/Montagnard_(Vietnam)

[74] "Khmer Krom", Wikipedia, last accessed September 23, 2023, https://en.wikipedia.org/wiki/Khmer_Krom

[75] Such as *R.C. v. District School Board of Niagara*, 2013 HRTO 1382 (CanLII) and *Rand v. Sealy Eastern Ltd.* (1982), 3 C.H.R.R. D/938 (Ont. Bd. Inq.)

Commission, unlawful discrimination because of religion can include:

> *Refusing to make an exception to dress codes to recognize religious dress requirements;*

> *Refusing to allow individuals to observe periods of prayer at particular times during the day;*

> *Refusing to permit individuals to take time off to observe a religious holiday.*

Therefore, Canadian employers are obligated to provide accommodations to employees who need the flexibility to fulfill the practice of their religious beliefs.

Since Indigenous peoples may not identify their spiritual beliefs as a religion, some jurisdictions (such as Ontario) use creed to include Indigenous spirituality under human rights protection. Several provisions in UNDRIP directly relate to rights associated with practicing Indigenous spirituality, including but not limited to the following:[76]

> *Article 12(1): Indigenous peoples have the right to manifest, practise, develop and teach their spiritual and religious traditions, customs and ceremonies; the right to maintain, protect, and have access in privacy to their religious and*

---

[76] "Resolution adopted by the General Assembly on 13 September 2007", United Nations, last accessed September 23, 2023, https://undocs.org/A/RES/61/295

cultural sites; the right to the use and control of their ceremonial objects; and the right to the repatriation of their human remains.

Article 25: Indigenous peoples have the right to maintain and strengthen their distinctive spiritual relationship with their traditionally owned or otherwise occupied and used lands, territories, waters and coastal seas and other resources and to uphold their responsibilities to future generations in this regard.

Article 34: Indigenous peoples have the right to promote, develop and maintain their institutional structures and their distinctive customs, spirituality, traditions, procedures, practices and, in the cases where they exist, juridical systems or customs, in accordance with international human rights standards.

Ableism

According to the World Health Organization (WHO), over one billion people worldwide live with some form of disability, and the number is increasing.[77] The World Health

---

[77] "Disability", World Health Organization, last accessed September 23, 2023, https://www.who.int/health-topics/disability#tab=tab_1

Organization (WHO) defines disability as an umbrella term for impairments, activity limitations and participation restrictions.[78]

Impairment affects a person's body structure and physical or mental functions. Examples of impairments include loss of a limb, loss of vision or loss of memory. Activity limitation includes difficulty seeing, hearing, walking, or problem-solving. Participation restriction affects a person's normal daily activities, such as working, engaging in social and recreational activities, and obtaining health care and preventive services.[79]

When addressing people with disabilities, WHO uses the term "*people with disability*" instead of "*persons with disabilities*" to extend it outside a minority group. [80] It is because chronic health conditions may also lead to disability; therefore, almost everyone is likely to experience some form of disability, temporary or permanent, at some point in life.[81]

---

[78] "Measuring Health and Disability, Manual for WHO Disability Assessment Schedule, WHODAS 2.0", World Health Organization, last accessed September 23, 2023, https://www.who.int/standards/classifications/international-classification-of-functioning-disability-and-health/who-disability-assessment-schedule

[79] "Disability and Health Overview", Centers for Disease Control and Prevention, last updated September 16, 2020, https://www.cdc.gov/ncbddd/disabilityandhealth/disability.html

[80] "Disability: People with disability vs persons with disabilities", World Health Organization, last updated December 7, 2020, https://www.who.int/news-room/q-a-detail/people-with-disability-vs-persons-with-disabilities

[81] "Disability and health", World Health Organization, last updated December 1, 2020, https://www.who.int/news-room/fact-sheets/detail/disability-and-health

There are different types of disabilities: physical movement limitations, memory problems, learning difficulties, mental disorders, hearing issues, vision disabilities, epilepsy, mental health disabilities, drug addictions, environmental sensitivities, difficulties in communication and social relationships, and other conditions. Many common diseases and addictions have been ruled to be the grounds of discrimination based on "disabilities" under their human rights code in many jurisdictions. They include but are not limited to acne,[82] alcoholism,[83] allergies and asthma,[84] diabetes,[85] migraine headaches,[86] and obesity.[87]

Different courts, tribunals, human rights acts and codes may have different interpretations of the term "disability". For example, the Canadian Human Rights Act defines disability as *any previous or existing mental or physical disability, including disfigurement and previous or existing dependence on alcohol or drugs.*

The Alberta Human Rights Act[88] defines "mental disability" as *any mental disorder, developmental disorder or*

---

[82] *De Jong and Horlacher Holdings Ltd* (1989), 10 C.H.R.R. D/6283 (B.C.H.R.C.)
[83] *Milazzo v. Autocar Connaisseur Inc. et al.*, 2003 CHRT 37 (CanLII)
[84] *Wachal v. Manitoba Pool Elevators*, 2000 CanLII 28872 (CHRT)
[85] *Brown v. Canadian Armed Forces*, 1995 CanLII 922 (CHRT)
[86] *Desormeaux v. Ottawa-Carleton Regional Transit*, 2003 CHRT 2 (CanLII)
[87] *Rogal v. Dalgleish* [2000] BCHRTD No. 22; *Dunlop v. Find and Kutzner* (No. 2), 2008 BCHRT 350
[88] "Alberta Human Rights Act", Alberta Queen's Printer, last accessed September 23, 2023, https://www.qp.alberta.ca/documents/Acts/A25P5.pdf

learning disorder, regardless of the cause or duration of the disorder, and "physical disability" as *any degree of physical disability, infirmity, malformation or disfigurement that is caused by bodily injury, birth defect or illness.* The Ontario Human Rights Code[89] has similar definitions with one additional category to cover other cases that may be omitted but fall under the act for worker's compensation.

However, so far, no human rights law includes protection for "normal ailments" as disabilities, such as flu or cold, where the effects have no permanence or impairment. In *Newfoundland (Human Rights Commission) v. Health Care Corp. of St. John's,*[90] the complainant alleged that the employer had discriminated against her on the basis of physical disability when it failed to promote her. The employer's position was that the complainant took about 480 days of sick leave in her 20 years of employment due to severe though unrelated medical conditions, which was the maximum sick leave available. As a result, the employer decided not to promote her because her absences constituted a continuing degree of unreliability, jeopardizing the leadership and coordinating functions she would be responsible for. The human rights tribunal decided that the complainant was not "disabled" as defined by the Ontario Human Rights Code.

---

[89] "Human Rights Code, R.S.O. 1990, c. H.19", Government of Ontario, last accessed September 23, 2023, https://www.ontario.ca/laws/statute/90h19
[90] 2001 CanLII 37580 (NL SC)

Family Status

There are different definitions for family status. In Western countries, it refers to whether a person has children or other dependents or not, including parents, grandparents and siblings. Sometimes, it also includes the marital status, such as single or partnered. It is more relevant when a person applies for rental housing than other matters.

People with children have a harder time renting than a couple or single persons because many landlords consider children annoying and naughty enough to cause damage to their property. The status of having children, especially during pregnancy, was also discriminated against by some employers. Such discrimination is sometimes classified as sex discrimination and sometimes as family status discrimination.

In a case that involved discrimination against pregnant women,[91] the Supreme Court of Canada made a statement, "...those who bear children and benefit society as a whole thereby should not be economically or socially disadvantaged seems to bespeak the obvious". Having children should not be considered as a disadvantage, both before and after the children are born.

In Hong Kong, "family status" means *the status of having responsibility for the care of an immediate family member*, and "immediate family member", in turn, means *a*

---

[91] *Brooks v. Canada Safeway Ltd.*, 1989 CanLII 96 (SCC), [1989] 1 SCR 1219

person who is related to someone by blood, marriage, adoption or affinity. It is a more restrictive definition which refers to the status of having responsibility for the care of an immediate family member only.

However, a more generous and liberal interpretation was given by the court in the case *Law Miu Kuen Sally v Sunbase International (Holdings) Limited,*[92] which includes marital status in the definition of family status.

Other Issues

There are other grounds for discrimination: ethnic origin, colour, sexual orientation, gender identity or expression, marital status, family status, genetic characteristics, receipt of public assistance and conviction for an offence.

Ethnic Origin

While a race is a group of people with the same physical characteristics that they are perceived to share, such as skin colour and eye shape,[93] an ethnic group is the people who have the same national, racial, cultural origins or state of belonging to such a group.[94]

---

[92] DCEO 7/2012

[93] "race", Cambridge Dictionary, last accessed September 23, 2023, https://dictionary.cambridge.org/dictionary/english/race

[94] "ethnicity", Cambridge Dictionary, last accessed May 28, 2021, https://dictionary.cambridge.org/dictionary/english/ethnicity

For example, Chinese, Japanese and Korean belong to the same race — East Asian, but there are different ethnic groups within China — Han, Miao, Tibetan, Uigur, and more. In fact, there are more than fifty ethnic groups in China. In Canada, there are more than 250 ethnic origins.[95]

Colour

In interracial marriages, people in the same ethnic group may have different skin, hair or eye colours. After a hundred years or so, those colours may still be different, but it is impossible to tell those different ethnic groups as every other trait is the same except colours. Sometimes, such difference is also referred to as different ancestry. However, ancestry discrimination may happen between two groups of people whose ethnicity is the same, whose colours are the same, but whose ancestors are not the same.

Sexual Orientation, Gender Identity or Expression

The direction of one's sexual interest or attraction can be different. It covers the range of human sexuality from lesbian and gay to bisexual and heterosexual. Historically, non-heterosexual people are often suppressed and discriminated against by people who are heterosexual. Even today, many members of the lesbian and gay community are

---

[95] "Ethnic and cultural origins of Canadians: Portrait of a rich heritage" Statistics Canada, last updated October 25, 2017, https://www12.statcan.gc.ca/census-recensement/2016/as-sa/98-200-x/2016016/98-200-x2016016-eng.cfm

still afraid to disclose their sexual orientation due to peer pressure or stereotypes from society.

While sexual orientation is about the sexual interest or attraction to a third party, gender identity or expression is about the person himself, herself or themselves. A person may be identified as female, male or both, regardless of the biological gender. They can also express their gender through clothing, behaviour, and personal appearance. As members of the LGBT group, people with a sex identity or expression other than their assigned sex at birth are often not accepted and discriminated against by many people.

Marital Status

The marital status of a person may refer to single, married, divorced, widowed, remarried, same-sex marriage, common-law marriage, or cohabitating couples. Historically, people would discriminate against individuals who were divorced, remarried or single after a certain age, not to mention those who were cohabitating couples and same-sex couples without legal status at the time.

Genetic Characteristics

Some people have a gene mutation that may cause or increase the risk of an inherited disorder. As a result, they are treated differently by their employer or insurance company because of the higher risk of having a disorder. Some jurisdictions have specific legislation to prohibit discrimination based on genetic characteristics.

Receipt of Public Assistance

People who receive public assistance are often stereotyped as lazy, with no commitment to their jobs, problematic, or unreliable. Like family status, it is more relevant when a person applies for rental housing than other matters and the recipients are often discriminated against by the landlords.

A Conviction for an Offence

People with a conviction for an offence are often in an inferior position, especially when they search for jobs. Many employers do not want to hire people with a criminal record, even if a pardon has been granted. People with a criminal record should not be discriminated against, at least not in employment-related issues.

As the law is constantly changing, there may be other grounds that cause discrimination and are overlooked. They may be fixed when a new law is made, or the existing laws are amended. For example, when same-sex marriage was illegal in Canada, there had been cases ruled by the tribunals that spouses and marital status definitions limited to opposite-sex couples were discriminatory.[96] The Supreme Court of Canada also ruled that the opposite-sex definition of "spouse" violated Section 15(1) of the Charter of Freedom.[97] After same-sex marriage became legal in Canada in 2005, the

---

[96] Such as *Leshner v. Ontario* (2) (1992), 16 C. H. R. R. D/ 184
[97] *M. v. H.*, 1999 CanLII 686 (SCC), [1999] 2 SCR 3

issues around same-sex couples[98] have significantly been reduced.

---

[98] Such as cases *Egan v. Canada*, 1995 CanLII 98 (SCC), [1995] 2 SCR 513 and *Halpern v. Canada (Attorney general)*, 2003 CanLII 26403 (ON CA)

3. Misconceptions

Most discriminations are due to misunderstanding and stereotyping. It starts with believing that one group of people is superior or inferior to other groups, hence developing discrimination.

Sexism

In the age of troglodytes, a good hunter had to be strong enough to fight with the animals using only stones and wooden spears. Males have a congenital advantage of more robustness and higher speed. Men who were good hunters became good fighters and leaders. Women were assigned to care for the children and do other non-hunting and non-combat work. Men started believing that they were superior to women and controlled them. That is why most of the societies in the world originated from patriarchal societies, which made males dominate those countries and states. However, that does not mean that women are less capable than men.

After the Industrial Revolution,[99] people did not rely on human forces as much as before. Using machines and equipment makes most work more accessible for both men and women, and both genders can perform the same quality

---

[99] "Industrial Revolution", Wikipedia, last accessed September 23, 2023, https://en.wikipedia.org/wiki/Industrial_Revolution

of work. Still, many people are biased and prefer hiring men over women. Some of them even set up unreasonable rules to raise the barriers to entry for women.

Most combats are now based on automatic assault rifles, missile launchers, and armoured cars carrying large calibre and turreted weapons systems in the military. Both men and women can operate them after having the same level of training. The operations of tanks, warships, submarines and fighter jets are also manageable by females. More and more captains of warships and commanders are female. However, sexism in the military still exists, and women often have to work hard to prove capable of doing the same tasks as men.

Ageism

Older adults are often stereotyped as not energetic, not creative and unreceptive to change. Other myths about older adults are well spread, such as older adults cannot learn new things.[100] Some top leaders in the world have refuted all such misconceptions or myths.

Both the 45th and 46th presidents of the United States are older adults when they run for their re-election and

---

[100] "10 Myths About Aging", National Institute on Aging, last accessed September 23, 2023, https://www.nia.nih.gov/health/10-myths-about-aging

election. Donald Trump[101] was 74 when he ran his re-election campaign, and Joe Biden[102] was 78 when he was elected. A report said that Donald Trump would run again in 2024 if he is healthy enough,[103] and most Republicans wanted him back.[104] Both US presidents showed that age is not a concern and that older adults can be energetic enough to run for an election.

Other top leaders in the world who won the election as older adults include Anerood Jugnauth,[105] Giorgio Napolitano[106] and Mahathir Mohamad.[107] Anerood Jugnauth was both President and Prime Minister of Mauritius. He was re-elected a few times and left the office at 86. Giorgio Napolitano ran his election campaign and was elected as the 11th President of Italy at 80 and left the office at 89. Mahathir Mohamad won the election in 2008 and became the 7th Prime

---

[101] "Donald Trump", Wikipedia, last accessed September 23, 2023, https://en.wikipedia.org/wiki/Donald_Trump

[102] "Joe Biden", Wikipedia, last accessed September 23, 2023, https://en.wikipedia.org/wiki/Joe_Biden

[103] "Trump has told associates he will run again in 2024 if he's healthy enough, report says", Business Insider, last updated May 27, 2021, https://www.businessinsider.com/trump-will-run-for-president-in-2024-if-healthy-politico-2021-5

[104] "Most Republicans Want Trump 2024, Other Candidates To Agree With Him: Poll", https://www.newsweek.com/most-republicans-want-donald-trump-2024-poll-1595378

[105] "Anerood Jugnauth", Wikipedia, last accessed September 23, 2023, https://en.wikipedia.org/wiki/Anerood_Jugnauth

[106] "Giorgio Napolitano", Wikipedia, last accessed September 23, 2023, https://en.wikipedia.org/wiki/Giorgio_Napolitano

[107] "Mahathir Mohamad", Wikipedia, last accessed September 23, 2023, https://en.wikipedia.org/wiki/Mahathir_Mohamad

Minister of Malaysia at 92. As of May 2021, he is still an active politician in Malaysia and the world.[108]

In business, old age is also not a hindrance for successful business owners. Warren Buffett,[109] CEO of Berkshire Hathaway and billionaire, is still managing his company as the chairman and CEO at the age of 90. Another billionaire, George Soros,[110] is also 90, managing his Soros Fund Management and is still active in stock trading.[111]

According to the National Bureau of Economic Research in the US, among the top 0.1% of startups,[112] the average age of their founders is 45.[113] In contrast, typical business founders started their businesses at the age of 34.[114] Although older adults are not as physically strong as young

---

[108] "PM Imran Khan, Malaysia's Mahathir Mohamad discuss Palestine situation over phone", Geo News, last updated May 17,2021, https://www.geo.tv/latest/350426-pm-imran-khan-malaysias-mahathir-mohamad-discuss-palestine-situation-over-phone

[109] "Warren Buffett", Wikipedia, last accessed September 23, 2023, https://en.wikipedia.org/wiki/Warren_Buffett

[110] "George Soros", Wikipedia, last accessed September 23, 2023, https://en.wikipedia.org/wiki/George_Soros

[111] "Billionaire George Soros Picks Up These 3 "Strong Buy" Stocks", Nasdaq Inc, last updated May 28, 2021, https://www.nasdaq.com/articles/billionaire-george-soros-picks-up-these-3-strong-buy-stocks-2021-05-28

[112] Based on growth in their first five years

[113] "Research: The Average Age of a Successful Startup Founder Is 45", Harvard Business Review, last updated July 11, 2018, https://hbr.org/2018/07/research-the-average-age-of-a-successful-startup-founder-is-45

[114] "The Typical Unicorn Founder Started Their Business at 34", Bloomberg, last updated May 21, 2021, https://www.bloomberg.com/news/articles/2021-05-21/what-s-the-average-age-of-a-startup-founder-it-s-34-study-says

people, their experience is usually directly proportional to their age.

Racism

Racism happens when people discover another race that is different from their own. They spoke different languages and could not communicate well. As a result, one ethnic group might feel superior to the other ethnic groups. Modern racial discrimination probably started from the genocide of Indigenous people[115] when the British[116] and Spanish[117] colonized the Americas. Even today, there are still concerns about systemic discrimination and outright racism against Indigenous people.[118]

When people think that a particular ethnic group is superior or inferior to other groups, such a biased belief may not cause any discrimination but will cause unfair assessments of ability, especially for the purpose of

---

[115] "When Native Americans Were Slaughtered in the Name of 'Civilization'", A&E Television Networks, last updated August 16, 2019, https://www.history.com/news/native-americans-genocide-united-states

[116] "British colonization of the Americas", Wikipedia, last accessed September 23, 2023, https://en.wikipedia.org/wiki/British_colonization_of_the_Americas

[117] "Spanish colonization of the Americas", Wikipedia, last accessed September 23, 2023, https://en.wikipedia.org/wiki/Spanish_colonization_of_the_Americas

[118] "Human Rights", United Nations, last accessed September 23, 2023, https://www.un.org/development/desa/indigenouspeoples/mandated-areas1/human-rights.html

employment. For example, some people believe that all Chinese have better math skills than most ethnic groups, which is a misconception.

I am proud of my math skills, and people always praise me for that. As a Chinese Canadian raised in Hong Kong, I know my excellent math skills are not because of my ethnicity. First of all, not all Chinese have excellent math skills. Secondly, we may have good math skills, but not because of race or genes. Thirdly, we perform better at the elementary and high school levels but not outstanding at the university and post-graduate levels. Lastly, we are good at math because of our education system but not our genes.

China, Singapore, Macao and Hong Kong are the top four countries and regions in the Program for International Student Assessment.[119] Macao[120] and Hong Kong[121] are the special administrative regions of China, and 76% of the population in Singapore is Chinese ethnic[122]. Hence, it seems that the Chinese have an advantage in mathematics. However, such a good result is all because of our education systems. China and Singapore have the most notorious

---

[119] "PISA 2018 Worldwide Ranking – average score of mathematics, science and reading", Facts Maps, last accessed September 23, 2023, https://factsmaps.com/pisa-2018-worldwide-ranking-average-score-of-mathematics-science-reading/

[120] "Macau", Wikipedia, last accessed September 23, 2023, https://en.wikipedia.org/wiki/Macau

[121] "Hong Kong", Wikipedia, last accessed September 23, 2023, https://en.wikipedia.org/wiki/Hong_Kong

[122] "Singapore", Wikipedia, last accessed September 23, 2023, https://en.wikipedia.org/wiki/Singapore

examination systems in the world, and students are loaded with exercises and tutorials every day.[123] [124] Another reason for the excellent performance of Chinese students is that we all have to memorize the multiplication table[125] when we are kids.

Fields Medal is regarded as the highest honours a mathematician can receive and is described as the Nobel Prize for mathematicians.[126] Only two are ethnic Chinese among all medal recipients,[127] and only one was educated in Hong Kong, China.[128] Mathematics may be the only science subject that does not need expensive and advanced equipment to do experiments. If the Chinese have better genes in mathematics, it will be reflected in the number of top mathematicians. The number of Fields medalists per capita in China is only 0.1, which is the lowest among all recipient countries.

[123] "Cram schools in Hong Kong", Wikipedia, last accessed September 23, 2023, https://en.wikipedia.org/wiki/Cram_schools_in_Hong_Kong

[124] "China planning new crackdown on private tutoring sector - sources", Reuters, last updated May 12, 2021, https://www.reuters.com/business/finance/exclusive-china-planning-new-crackdown-private-tutoring-sector-sources-2021-05-12/

[125] "Chinese multiplication table", Wikipedia, last accessed September 23, 2023, https://en.wikipedia.org/wiki/Chinese_multiplication_table

[126] "Fields Medal", Wikipedia, last accessed September 23, 2023, https://en.wikipedia.org/wiki/Fields_Medal

[127] "Fields Medal for Mathematics Per Capita", areppim AG, last updated November 2, 2020, https://stats.areppim.com/stats/stats_fieldsxcapita.htm

[128] "Shing-Tung Yau", Wikipedia, last accessed September 23, 2023, https://en.wikipedia.org/wiki/Shing-Tung_Yau

We cannot say that the Chinese have no advantages in mathematics, especially business mathematics. However, we have the advantage because of our training and education, not our genes. In other words, students of other ethnic groups receive the same kind of training and education as the Chinese students received in China and Singapore should get the same performance in the mathematics assessments.

On the other hand, a student from a tropical country said that people stereotyped them as a lazy ethnic group. The student admitted that most people in that country are unwilling to work, as their lifestyle is to enjoy their lives rather than chase money and fame. The tropical country has rich resources. People have fruit trees in their backyards, and it is effortless to fish at the beaches. That is the dream of many people in developed countries for their retirement life. The supply of food seems unlimited, and people are satisfied with the status quo. That is why they are not willing to work. However, their lifestyle changed when they immigrated to Canada. All the fellow immigrants from that country work very hard in Canada to make a living.

Actually, anyone born and lives in that country, regardless of their ethnic origin, may not want to work hard because of the lifestyle, and it is easy to make a living. That is one of the reasons why all developed countries do not have social welfare to support their citizens to enjoy lives materially without working. It is the environment that makes people not want to work, not their genes. Therefore, the accusation of laziness of any ethnic group is a kind of serious racism and should not be allowed.

The communist countries have all learned a lesson, too. China[129], Vietnam[130] and Cuba[131] have all changed their economic structures. Before the economic reform in 1978, the Chinese economy was dominated by state ownership and central planning, and most workers received the same level of wages regardless of their performance. As a result, people did not want to work hard as there was no incentive for hardworking people, and the economic performance was terrible.

Some say that one of the Chinese traits is that we all work hard,[132] but the economic system between 1949 and 1978 disrupted such a trait. Therefore, it is fair to say that the Chinese's hardworking trait is created by education and culture, such as Confucianism, but not our genes. Like math skills, hard work can be conditioned and become a culture after thousands of years, especially going through famines. Any ethnic group can develop a particular culture, including hardworking, although it takes time.

---

[129] "Chinese economic reform", Wikipedia, last accessed September 23, 2023, https://en.wikipedia.org/wiki/Chinese_economic_reform

[130] "Đổi Mới", Wikipedia, last accessed September 23, 2023, https://en.wikipedia.org/wiki/%C4%90%E1%BB%95i_M%E1%BB%9Bi

[131] "Economy of Cuba", Wikipedia, last accessed September 23, 2023, https://en.wikipedia.org/wiki/Economy_of_Cuba

[132] "Why are the Chinese workers known as the most hard working workers in the world?", Quora, last updated May 19, 2021, https://www.quora.com/Why-are-the-Chinese-workers-known-as-the-most-hard-working-workers-in-the-world

Creed

Religion is a deep, complex and challenging subject. Many scholars in theology spent their whole lives studying just one religion but still could not know it thoroughly. Ordinary people either believe in the religion they picked and learned about or have no religious beliefs. Therefore, people of different religions may have many misunderstandings about religions other than their beliefs.

Take Christians, for example; some Protestant Christians[133] criticize Catholic Christians[134] who worship idols, and the Holy Mary is one of them. The allegations were based on a misunderstanding. Those people missed the explanation from the Catholic Church — devotion to the Holy Mary does not amount to worship, which is reserved for God. The tradition of the Catholic Church views the Holy Mary as subordinate to Christ, but she is seen as above all other creatures.[135] Catholic Christians do not worship the Holy Mary but just commemorate her.

---

[133] "Protestantism", Wikipedia, last accessed September 23, 2023, https://en.wikipedia.org/wiki/Protestantism
[134] "Catholic Church", Wikipedia, last accessed September 23, 2023, https://en.wikipedia.org/wiki/Catholic_Church
[135] "Marian devotions", Wikipedia, last accessed September 23, 2023, https://en.wikipedia.org/wiki/Marian_devotions

Although Roman Catholicism, Anglo-Catholicism,[136] High Church Lutheranism,[137] Eastern Orthodoxy,[138] Oriental Orthodoxy[139] and Protestant churches share the same belief in the divinity of Jesus Christ, there are differences among those groups. If people are not believers in a particular religion, they will not go to study groups, worship ceremonies, or gatherings in that religion. Misunderstandings may happen and cannot be solved without communication or first-hand experience.

Different groups that share the same belief, such as Christianity, can still have misunderstandings. Believers in one religion may misunderstand another religion easily. Even for people with no religious belief, when they face a strange religion and do not have the opportunity to learn about it, misunderstandings can also quickly occur, and discrimination will result.

---

[136] "Anglo Catholicism", Wikipedia, last accessed September 23, 2023, https://en.wikipedia.org/wiki/Anglo-Catholicism

[137] "High church Lutheranism", Wikipedia, last accessed September 23, 2023, https://en.wikipedia.org/wiki/High_church_Lutheranism

[138] "Eastern Orthodox Church", Wikipedia, last accessed September 23, 2023, https://en.wikipedia.org/wiki/Eastern_Orthodox_Church

[139] "Oriental Orthodox Churches", Wikipedia, last accessed September 23, 2023, https://en.wikipedia.org/wiki/Oriental_Orthodox_Churches

Other than Christianity, there are many other religions worldwide, such as Hinduism,[140] Islam[141] and Buddhism.[142] Among them, there are many branches and different practices. Religious freedom is protected in most countries, especially those committed to protecting human rights. In a religiously free society, people have the freedom to believe or not believe in a religion. However, we do not have the right to force other people to accept our faith or go against a particular belief. Unfortunately, religious antisemitism,[143] persecution of Christians[144] and Islamophobia still happen in many countries.

Ableism

There are many myths about people with disabilities, such as that *they have a higher absentee rate than employees without disabilities* and that *other employees will always have to help them*. Such biased comments are not uncommon in the workplace, but the facts have proven that they are wrong.

---

[140] "Hinduism", Wikipedia, last accessed September 23, 2023, https://en.wikipedia.org/wiki/Hinduism

[141] "Islam", Wikipedia, last accessed September 23, 2023, https://en.wikipedia.org/wiki/Islam

[142] "Buddhism", Wikipedia, last accessed September 23, 2023, https://en.wikipedia.org/wiki/Buddhism

[143] "Religious antisemitism", Wikipedia, last accessed September 23, 2023, https://en.wikipedia.org/wiki/Religious_antisemitism

[144] "Persecution of Christians", Wikipedia, last accessed September 23, 2023, https://en.wikipedia.org/wiki/Persecution_of_Christians

According to the studies done by DuPont Corporation in 1993, scholars Adams-Shollenberger and Mitchell in 1996, Blanck and Braddock in 1998 and Olsen, Cioffi, Yovanoff, and Mank in 2001,[145] on average, individuals with disabilities have better attendance rates than their non-disabled counterparts.

Helping co-workers is a common practice in the workplace. Not only the people with disabilities may need help from others, but everyone may. On the other hand, it depends on the type of work; people with disabilities may perform better than non-disabled colleagues. Many employees with disabilities do not need any assistance from their colleagues to perform their jobs. Even if they do, the assistance they require can be neglectable compared to the work they contribute.

Take Stephen Hawking[146] as an example. He was diagnosed with Amyotrophic Lateral Sclerosis (ALS) in 1963. ALS causes degeneration of motor neurons in the brain and interferes with messages to muscles in the body. As a result, it gradually paralyzed him over the decades. However, Hawking's outstanding contribution to the science field is undebatable.

---

[145] "People with disabilities: A new model of productive labor", University of New Hampshire Scholars' Repository, last accessed September 23, 2023, https://scholars.unh.edu/cgi/viewcontent.cgi?article=1017&context=hospman_facpub

[146] "Stephen Hawking", Wikipedia, last accessed September 23, 2023, https://en.wikipedia.org/wiki/Stephen_Hawking

A software developer who relies on a wheelchair to get around will not need any assistance from co-workers to do the programming work. A truck driver with communication difficulties will not have any problems at work due to such an issue. There are countless examples to show that people with disabilities can perform the same quality of work as people with no disability or even better. Stevie Wonder[147] is another excellent example.

With the improvement of assistant equipment, such as electric wheelchairs, lighter prostheses and powered exoskeletons,[148] physical movements will no longer limit the productivity of persons with disabilities. With suitable accommodations, persons with disabilities can perform work the same way as non-disabled people; even people with ALS, like Hawking, can do their job well.[149]

Most Paralympic contestants performed better than ordinary people without disabilities. Some of them can even compete in both the Paralympics and the Olympics.[150]

---

[147] "Stevie Wonder", Wikipedia, last accessed September 23, 2023, https://en.wikipedia.org/wiki/Stevie_Wonder

[148] "Powered exoskeleton", Wikipedia, last accessed September 23, 2023, https://en.wikipedia.org/wiki/Powered_exoskeleton

[149] "Dr. Stephen Hawking: A Case Study on Using Technology to Communicate with the World", University of Washington, last accessed September 23, 2023, https://www.washington.edu/accesscomputing/dr-stephen-hawking-case-study-using-technology-communicate-world

[150] "List of athletes who have competed in the Paralympics and Olympics", Wikipedia, last accessed September 23, 2023, https://en.wikipedia.org/wiki/List_of_athletes_who_have_competed_in_the_Paralympics_and_Olympics

Therefore, people with disabilities may perform average and even better than ordinary people, with or without equipment to assist them.

Family Status

When a person needs to take care of a family member, such a person is often stereotyped as inflexible during work hours, cannot work on duty or on shifts, and will affect job performance. Many employers believe that taking care of a family member would hinder the performance of their employees.

Many people also think that children are annoying and could cause damage to their property, and mature singles are difficult to get along with, which is why they are single. Some people also see a failed marriage as a reflection of the flawed character of a person.

Other Issues

There are also misconceptions about other groups of people, such as the LGBT group, families with kids and people with criminal records. Statistics and education may help eliminate negative attitudes and feelings toward those people.

4. Equity

Equity is based on diversity and inclusion to provide fair and respectful treatment of all people regardless of their background. It creates opportunities for diverse communities and reduces disparities in opportunities. Ultimately, it leads to equitable outcomes for them. Equity is achieved by removing systemic barriers and biases so that all individuals with different backgrounds will have equal opportunities to access and benefit from a program, such as employment, education and government programs.

The foundation of equity is human rights. While human rights are the basic protections of citizens and are governed by laws, equity in EDI policy is a voluntary goal to be achieved. In most Western countries, the governments have consolidated laws to protect human rights. For example, the federal government of Canada passed the Canadian Human Rights Act. At the same time, most of its provinces also have their only law to interpret human rights for better protection from their points of view.

Hong Kong has no consolidated legislation to protect all kinds of human rights. Instead, Hong Kong has four ordinances to protect certain rights. They are the Sex Discrimination Ordinance (Cap. 480), the Disability Discrimination Ordinance (Cap. 487), the Family Status Discrimination Ordinance (Cap. 527) and the Race

Discrimination Ordinance (Cap. 602). However, there is no legislation to protect people from age and religious discrimination yet.

We must keep in mind that equity is not an absolute measure or supply of opportunities nor a proportional outcome based on the population of a community. For example, male and female athletes will not compete in the same event unless it is a team match, such as a mixed game for men and women. That is because there are differences between the physical characteristics of males and females.

Equality is provided for people to access a program to have a fair opportunity to participate. It is not a guarantee of outcome based on the absolute ratio of the diverse groups in the community. Unfortunately, many people use the outcome on the surface to tell if equity has been achieved.

Employment

As discussed in *Chapdelaine v. Air Canada*, the airline rejected a group of females because they failed to meet the minimum height requirement of five feet and six inches. Now, most employers in Canada have no physical requirements such as minimum height or good eyesight, as the employees can use equipment to assist them. Even the federal,[151]

---

[151] "Physical standards to become an RCMP officer", Royal Canadian Mounted Police, last updated May 30, 2019, https://www.rcmp-grc.gc.ca/en/physical-standards

provincial,[152] and municipal[153] police forces have no minimum height, weight and eyesight requirements. That is not the case in Hong Kong.

The physical requirements for joining the Hong Kong Police are:

You must have a good physique, as you will be required to pass a physical fitness test during the selection process. If you are a male candidate, you should be at least 163cm tall and weigh 50kg. For female candidates, you must be at least 152cm tall and weigh 42kg. You must have good eyesight, and you are required to pass an initial eyesight test without the aid of any eyesight correction tools.[154]

Like the *Chapdelaine v. Air Canada* case, these physical requirements are discriminative. All employers in Hong Kong, including the government, should be sensitive to possible discrimination and remove those unnecessary

---

[152] "Uniform Recruitment", Ontario Provincial Police, last updated October 26 2021 https://www.opp.ca/index.php?id=115&entryid=56b7c5868f94acaf5c28d17d

[153] "Police Constable and Cadets", Peel Regional Police, last accessed September 23, 2023, https://www.peelpolice.ca/en/work-with-us/police-constable-and-cadets.aspx

[154] "Entry Requirements", The Hong Kong Police, last accessed September 23, 2023, https://www.police.gov.hk/ppp_en/15_recruit/er.html

requirements. There is room for employers in Hong Kong to protect human rights better and improve their EDI policies.

In *Tsang Helen v Cathay Pacific Airways Ltd*,[155] the plaintiff was employed by the defendant as a female flight attendant. According to the defendant's retirement policy, the female cabin crew needed to retire at 40 years old, while males could work until the age of 55. Male flight attendants were in a much better position than female flight attendants, and the only reason for this difference was their gender. The court ruled that it was direct discrimination under the Sex Discrimination Ordinance.

In another case,[156] three plaintiffs applied for the posts of ambulance paramedic, firefighter and customs officer, respectively, in the Fire Services Department and the Customs and Excise Department. Their offers of employment were either withheld or terminated following offers of conditional employment because they had a parent with mental illness. Although both Departments have a policy that job applicants with a first-degree relative with a history of mental illness of a hereditary nature would be rejected, the court ruled that the two Departments had discriminated against the plaintiffs on the grounds of the mental illness of their relatives, disability of an associate under s. 6(c) of the Disability Discrimination Ordinance.

---

[155] DCEO 5/2000
[156] *K & Ors v Secretary for Justice*, DCEO 3, 4 and 7/1999

One of the most important things people care about in their careers is their chances of promotion. Suppose there are ten people in a team, and there are five supervisor positions for their promotion. In that case, no one will expect all team members to be promoted to supervisors. That is, equity is not to provide equal outcomes to everyone. If there are six males and four females in the team, the outcome should not be based on the ratio. That is, getting promoted should not always be three males and two females.

The same logic applies to different groups. If there are six white persons and four black persons in that team, the promotion should not be based on the ethnic ratio so that three white persons and two black persons get the promotion. When there are more groups in the team, such as youths and older adults, with and without disabilities, or married and single, no proportional outcome can be made to 'fairly' accommodate each group.

Even based on a proportional population, it can only achieve absolute equity but not true equity, and the result may not please any group in the community. A retired sub-lieutenant of the Royal Canadian Navy told me about an unwritten rule in the Navy before his retirement. The rule was that the number of commissioned officers in each grade should be 70% British Canadians and 30% French Canadians, which was the approximate proportion of British and French Canadians in the total population of Canada at the time.

The sub-lieutenant said none of the navy officers were pleased with such a convention. He said the purpose of the rule was to protect the promotion opportunities of French Canadians, being a minority, in the navy. The failure of the rule was due to the absolute ratio used, not an objective assessment of the ability of the officers. Assuming that there was no other minority in the Canadian navy at that time, such a rule still could not reasonably protect the interests of both British and French Canadians.

All kinds of promotions should be based on the performance of the individuals first. It is the same in the Navy or corporations. Rigidly fixing the ratio of promotion based on the distribution of populations is unfair to each ethnic group. While the French Canadians might believe they had more cadets capable of being promoted to officers than the allowed 30% quota, the British Canadians might also think they deserved more than 70% of the chances. That is why such a policy can never satisfy each ethnic group.

For promotions in employment, the decisions should be made based mainly on the performance of the employees but not their ethnicity, gender or creed. The same logic should also be applied to education and other programs. To assist those groups with historical disadvantages, we can give merits to them objectively, according to a points system based on statistics. That will be discussed in Chapter 7.

Education

Equity in education does not mean that teachers will teach in all languages or use the same method to facilitate and deliver the materials to all students. Instead, educational resources should be allocated based on individual needs. For example, students with vision or hearing impairment need special equipment to assist them in learning, which will not be used by or supplied to all students.

The concept of absolute equity is also found in the education field. Some universities set a minimum quota to accept minority students in their most popular subjects, such as medicine, engineering and law. They have spots reserved for certain ethnicities to ensure that they have access to acquire those degrees as per the concept of equity. Such an absolute assignment of admission spots will do more harm than good.

The Hong Kong government used a system to place students in secondary schools depending in part on gender. Boys and girls were treated separately in the scaling process with different scaling curves. As a result, girls needed a higher score for better schools than boys. Moreover, there was a gender quota in co-educational secondary schools to ensure that a fixed ratio of boys and girls would be admitted to each school. The Equal Opportunities Commission challenged the legality of the system by way of judicial review.[157] The court held that the operation of the system amounted to unlawful direct discrimination against students on the basis of sex under the Sex Discrimination Ordinance.

All professional practitioners have to achieve a minimum qualification for their licenses, as their quality of services may cause public safety. An unqualified doctor may cause medical malpractice that can be fatal. An incompetent architect or civil engineer may cause buildings or structures to collapse, resulting in a disaster. Universities are gatekeepers to ensure that those professionals are well-trained and qualified to meet the minimum standard. Such a standard should not be lowered just for the purpose of accepting a larger cohort of students from a specific ethnic group. The bottom line is that it cannot sacrifice public safety.

On the other hand, some universities[158] have already been accused of using numerus clausus[159] to cap the number of students of some ethnic groups, such as Asian[160] and

---

[157] *Equal Opportunities Commission v Director of Education*, HCAL 1555/2000

[158] "Ivy League Exhibits Anti-Asian Bias", Manhattan Institute for Policy Research, last updated March 9, 2016, https://www.city-journal.org/html/fewer-asians-need-apply-14180.html

[159] "Numerus clausus", Wikipedia, last accessed September 23, 2023, https://en.wikipedia.org/wiki/Numerus_clausus

[160] "Asian quota", Wikipedia, last accessed September 23, 2023, https://en.wikipedia.org/wiki/Asian_quota

Jewish.[161] It was said that Asian students need SAT[162] scores 140 points higher than white students, 270 points higher than Hispanic students, and 450 points higher than black students to enter famous private universities.[163][164]

The word "university" is derived from the Latin "*universitas magistrorum et scholarium*", which means "community of teachers and scholars".[165] Unlike corporations that hire employees, which need other types of assets to fit into the positions, such as experience and personal connections, universities are the places for students to learn and develop their knowledge; they should mainly be based on academic performance to accept the candidates. Students enter universities to learn and advance their knowledge. To ensure the students' success in learning, universities should make their acceptance criteria primarily based on students' academic results. If there are other reasons to be considered, they should assess the materials quantitatively but not simply based on ethnicity and ignore the academic achievements of other students. The details will be discussed in Chapter 7.

[161] "Jewish quota", Wikipedia, last accessed September 23, 2023, https://en.wikipedia.org/wiki/Jewish_quota

[162] "SAT", Wikipedia, last accessed September 23, 2023, https://en.wikipedia.org/wiki/SAT

[163] "Fewer Asians Need Apply", Manhattan Institute for Policy Research, last updated Winter, 2016, https://www.city-journal.org/html/fewer-asians-need-apply-14180.html

[164] "Letter-asians-need-to-score-140-points-higher-than-white-applicants", Wikipedia, last accessed September 23, 2023, https://www.mercurynews.com/2020/06/23/letter-asians-need-to-score-140-points-higher-than-white-applicants/

[165] "University", Wikipedia, last accessed September 23, 2023, https://en.wikipedia.org/wiki/University

Raising the barriers to entry to limit a particular ethnic group from entering the universities is unfair to that group unless an objective measure is used. We should not sacrifice the rights of one ethnic group to help another group. That violates the basic principles of equity. If there is an ethnic group that needs help, we should assist that particular group but not restrain other groups and give that particular group the advantages.

The low acceptance rate of a particular ethnic group, such as the Indigenous people, to medical schools or universities is due to many reasons, and poverty is one of them. Instead of offering special quotas for those ethnic groups, scholarships may be a better solution for certain disadvantaged groups.

To help the students of vulnerable groups, governments should carry out their equity, diversity and inclusion policies in all stages of education. All ethnic groups should be able to study in a welcoming and respectful environment, starting at the pre-school level. Suppose all ethnic groups can receive the same type of education and social services since they were born. In that case, the vulnerable groups will not have any disadvantages and can compete on a fair platform at every stage. All service providers, including elementary and high schools, shall provide equity to vulnerable groups to achieve better academic results so that universities do not have to play the role of the final gatekeeper.

A report shows that 98.3% of the students enrolled in medical schools in Canada eventually graduated.[166] That means once a medical school in Canada accepts the students, their graduations are almost "guaranteed". It is, therefore, crucial to ensure fairness in taking university and medical school students.

In *Law Chi Yuen (formerly known as Law O Ki) by Wong Sin, his next friend, v Secretary for Education*,[167] the applicant suffered from an intellectual disability and studied in a primary-level special school in Hong Kong for students with intellectual disabilities. The Education Bureau (EDB) rejected his school's application to join the Hong Kong Government's Native-speaking English Teacher ("NET") Scheme because EDB claimed that he had different educational needs. Thus, the NET Scheme did not cover his School.

The court found that a primary-level student without any disability, under the curriculum of a mainstream school, could enjoy the benefits of full-time NETs. In contrast, the plaintiff could only have a peripatetic NET acting as an Advisory Teacher and visiting his school only several times a year. The court ruled that the EDB discriminated against the plaintiff based on his intellectual disability. As a result, the EDB has to provide equal access to NET teachers in every

---

[166] "Investigating Canadian medical school attrition metrics to inform socially accountable admissions planning", National Library of Medicine. Last updated June 2, 2021, https://pubmed.ncbi.nlm.nih.gov/26037742/
[167] HCAL 91/2011; [2016] 5 HKLRD 302

school, regardless of whether their nature is mainstream or special needs.

Public Policy

It is common that a change in public policy is required to cut back on resources due to reduced budgets. Services like the operating hours of parks, swimming pools, daycare and community centres may have to be reduced. An absolute equity approach will cut the operating hours of each location in the same way, regardless of the needs of different communities.

In reality, there is a likely chance that people in less wealthy neighbourhoods use those municipal facilities more frequently than those in affluent neighbourhoods, who can afford access to private facilities. Therefore, reducing the hours in wealthier neighbourhoods may have fewer impacts on the residents as a whole.

In public housing, priorities are often given to vulnerable groups, including single parents, older adults and persons with disabilities. Of course, a low income level is often the prerequisite to applying for subsidized housing.

There are affordable housing programs tailored for Indigenous people in Canada,[168] but none in the United States.[169]

Equity in public housing schemes is more critical than in other services, as housing is a necessity. We have to ensure that all the applicants are fairly treated and assessed. For example, when there are two applicants from the same income level, one is an older adult over 80 of age, and one is a young person with disabilities, who should be prioritized for getting a unit? That should be quantified and will be discussed in Chapter 7.

In Canada,[170] the United States[171] and the United Kingdom,[172] there are tax allowances or tax credits for persons with disabilities, people with children dependents or under maternity. Those are the groups that are under the protection of the human rights code. However, not every

---

168 "Affordable housing in Ontario", Ministry of Municipal Affairs and Housing, last updated, July 20, 2020, https://www.ontario.ca/page/affordable-housing-ontario
169 "Hud's Public Housing Program", U.S. Department of Housing and Urban Development, last accessed September 23, 2023, https://www.hud.gov/topics/rental_assistance/phprog
170 "Disability tax credit (DTC)", Government of Canada, last updated January 18, 2021, https://www.canada.ca/en/revenue-agency/services/tax/individuals/segments/tax-credits-deductions-persons-disabilities/disability-tax-credit.html
171 "More Information for People with Disabilities", Internal Revenue Service, last updated December 7, 2020, https://www.irs.gov/individuals/more-information-for-people-with-disabilities
172 "Income Tax", Government of the United Kingdom, last accessed June 7, 2021, https://www.gov.uk/income-tax/taxfree-and-taxable-state-benefits

group under the human rights code has tax benefits, such as widowed parents, and not every group with tax benefits under the human rights code, such as veterans. It is difficult to achieve equity in taxation, even when progressive tax rates are used.

Sometimes, the government or authority is too lazy to correct the mistakes that cause inequality. For example, an old English law that makes females eating chocolate in public illegal still exists,[173] which is obviously discriminative.

In *Leung Kwok Hung, also known as "Long Hair", v Commissioner of Correctional Services*,[174] a male prisoner was required to have his hair cut pursuant to the Service Order of Hong Kong Correctional Services ("Standing Order") and applied for Judicial Review against the decision requiring him to cut his hair.

The Standing Order regulated the hair length of both male and female prisoners, but only male prisoners had to keep their hair cut "sufficiently close". In contrast, female prisoners' hair could only be cut shorter than her style upon admission to prison with her consent. The case escalated to the Court of Final Appeal, which held that the Standing Order constituted direct discrimination against the male prisoners. Consequently, the Correctional Services started cutting the

---

[173] "Strange English Laws", Solicitors North East, last updated August 18, 2016, https://solicitorsnortheast.co.uk/strange-english-laws/
[174] FACV 8/2019; [2020] HKCFA 37

hair of female prisoners after losing that court battle to achieve "equity".[175]

Other Issues

Another example of absolute equity is that some people name their children using both parents' last names. It is similar to the traditional double surname,[176] but the reason is not to preserve a surname. The new type of double surname is used to symbolize equity between the parents, as both want to show their family names through their children.

Suppose the parents are Lesley Doe and Sandy Smith; their children's last name will be Doe-Smith. Some people will name their children alternatively to extend the equity. In that case, the last name of the first child will be Doe-Smith, and the second child's last name will be Smith-Doe, and continue like that.

Keeping on using that type of naming method will cause problems in their later generations. The last name will exponentially expand if every generation uses the same naming method. When a person with the last name A-B

---

[175] "Hong Kong prisons start trimming female inmates' tresses just past shoulders after court ruling on sex discrimination", South China Morning Post, last updated February 13, 2021, https://www.scmp.com/news/hong-kong/law-and-crime/article/3121579/hong-kong-prisons-start-trimming-female-inmates

[176] "Double-barrelled name", Wikipedia, last accessed September 23, 2023, https://en.wikipedia.org/wiki/Double-barrelled_name

marries a person with the last name C-D, their children will be named A-B-C-D. When their child marries another person with the same naming method, whose last name is E-F-G-H, their fourth generation will have the last name A-B-C-D-E-F-G-H. It will be a nightmare for everyone who deals with such a long last name.

Sometimes, absolute equity can be done, but not in every single situation. For example, the word 'they' is used to replace 'he' and 'she' as gender neutrality[177] to promote equity between males and females. It can also eliminate the possibility of accidentally offending the LGBT group. However, it should be used with caution as it may not be suitable in some scenarios and create confusion. Below is an example.

An education provider wanted to promote equity by avoiding gender. However, their clients were English language schools that required students to practice comprehension. The company proposed to use "they" to replace "he" and "she" in all their course materials. The following exercise is similar to one of theirs in the material, which would create confusion:

> *Michael asked Mary for a date. They bought them dinner, and they kissed their cheeks.*

---

[177] "Gender neutrality in languages with gendered third-person pronouns", Wikipedia, last accessed September 23, 2023, https://en.wikipedia.org/wiki/Gender_neutrality_in_languages_with_gendered_third-person_pronouns

They went home at nine o'clock, and they
arrived home at ten.

1. *Who spent money on their date?*
2. *Who returned home earlier?*

The learner would not be able to answer the questions without knowing the gender of the pronouns in the contents. If we write it ordinarily, like most books that teach the English language, then the contents are crystal clear.

Michael asked Mary for a date. He bought her
dinner, and she kissed his cheek. She went
home at nine o'clock, and he went home at ten.

1. *Who spent money on their date?*
2. *Who returned home earlier?*

Answer 1: Michael
Answer 2: Mary

Equity should not be done just for political correctness, on the surface, and ignore the potential problems.

Most of the time, equity is done by giving vulnerable groups advantages so they have the same opportunities as others. Sometimes, preferential treatments are delivered directly to those vulnerable groups without going through assessments. For example, many merchants offer seniors over the age of 65 a discount or free admission to parks. That kind of treatment is called positive discrimination, which is legal and usually used as a "recognition".

The rationale is based on the fact that people over 65 have historically been subjected to discrimination. The same logic applies to ladies' night events in clubs or other types of preferential treatments. However, caution must be made when setting up such policies, especially based on other grounds not under the human rights code. The preferential treatments may cause constructive discrimination. Constructive discrimination is unintentional, but it singles out a group of people and results in unequal treatment.

Changing the outcomes or making decisions based solely on people's traits is risky and can be unfair. Positive discrimination should not be used in the selection process with limited resources. Dining in a restaurant can be classified as an unlimited supply as patronages just pay money to enjoy the food. A senior discount allows older adults to enjoy a discounted price or free of charge but not a privilege to be treated exceptionally, such as a table guarantee without reservation. Housing authorities and universities can offer a special rent or fee to a particular group. However, quotas in universities, public housing, and employment are limited. No one should award such a quota to a person just because that person belongs to a particular group without considering other measures unless the residence is built for such a purpose (such as senior homes).

It takes time to achieve better equity, and we need to push the governments to do more sooner and more proactively. For example, the United Nations General Assembly adopted the United Nations Declaration on the Rights of Indigenous Peoples (UNDRIP) in 2007, with a majority of 144 states favouring it and four voting against it.[178] The four countries that voted no were Australia, Canada, New Zealand, and the United States.

UNDRIP addresses individual and collective rights, cultural rights and identity, and rights to education, health, employment, language, and others. It protects Indigenous peoples' rights, including on issues relating to land, culture, identity, religion, language, health, education, governance and community. It is the most comprehensive instrument on the rights of Indigenous peoples all over the world. It establishes a universal framework of minimum standards for the Indigenous peoples' survival, dignity, and well-being. It elaborates on the existing human rights laws in all countries as they apply to Indigenous peoples' specific situations.

The four countries voted against it because they had Indigenous issues in their countries and thus were unwilling to support it. However, under the pressure of their citizens, lobbying groups, opposition parties or the change of

---

[178] "United Nations Declaration on the Rights of Indigenous Peoples", United Nations, last accessed September 23, 2023, https://www.un.org/development/desa/indigenouspeoples/declaration-on-the-rights-of-indigenous-peoples.html

governments, the four countries later all endorsed the declaration.

The Australian government was the first country among the four to endorse the UNDRIP in 2009 formally.[179] The New Zealand government approved[180] it just months later. Canada issued a Statement of Support[181] in 2010, endorsing the principles of UNDRIP. The government of the United States also endorsed UNDRIP with a formal announcement made in January 2011.[182]

To conclude, equity is not delivered automatically, and people must fight for it. It is not absolute and should not be measured by the outcomes. It should be measured by the mechanism of the selection process. However, many people will judge it on the surface. For example, it is easy to notice people's ethnicities, ages and genders but not their creeds,

---

[179] "Declaration on the Rights of Indigenous Peoples", Wikipedia, last accessed September 23, 2023, https://en.wikipedia.org/wiki/Declaration_on_the_Rights_of_Indigenous_Peoples

[180] "Ministerial Statements — UN Declaration on the Rights of Indigenous Peoples—Government Support", The New Zealand Parliament, last updated April 20, 2010, https://www.parliament.nz/en/pb/hansard-debates/rhr/document/49HansD_20100420_00000071/ministerial-statements-un-declaration-on-the-rights-of

[181] "ARCHIVED - Canada's Statement of Support on the United Nations Declaration on the Rights of Indigenous Peoples", Indigenous and Northern Affairs Canada, last accessed September 23, 2023, https://www.aadnc-aandc.gc.ca/eng/1309374239861/1309374546142

[182] "Announcement of U.S. Support for the United Nations Declaration on the Rights of Indigenous Peoples", The U.S. State Department, last updated January 12, 2011, https://2009-2017.state.gov/s/srgia/154553.htm

sexual orientations or family status. That makes some organizations put their emphasis on only race, age and gender, as the public quickly notices them. An in-depth approach based on statistics and a points system should be used to achieve true equity.

5. Diversity

The concept of diversity is to include as many different types of people as possible according to the demographics of the country or region. At first, it referred to age, gender and different ethnicities in the community or nation. Later, it includes different religions, family status, sexual orientation, marital status and more.

Diversity ensures that every group in society has access to the services or facilities, has an opportunity to be employed, accepted as students, or enjoys a benefit. In employment and education, diversity can improve the quality and performance of corporations and institutions by capturing the uniqueness and strengths of individuals with different backgrounds.

Diversity is also referred to accepting, helping or hiring people according to different traits such as race, age, colour, place of origin, religion, family and marital status, ethnic origin, ability, sex, sexual orientation, gender identity, gender expression—all the grounds for discrimination under the human rights code. It also includes education, citizenship, life experience, employment status, union affiliation, political beliefs and more. As long as they are human characteristics, they can be used to classify people into groups—even people who wear glasses and do not wear glasses or men who have a beard and without a beard can be classified as different groups.

The goal of diversity is to consider and serve as many different groups as possible, particularly those with historical disadvantages or who remain underrepresented. It respects individuals for their unique characteristics, strengths, talents, skills, and abilities, regardless of who they are. By recognizing everyone's uniqueness and specialty, diversity can bring more benefits to the collective.

Race

Under the same race, there are different ethnic groups and people with different colours or ancestors. There are only five defined races — American Indian, Malay, Ethiopian (later termed Negroid), Mongolian, and Caucasian.[183] Although they were proposed about 250 years ago, many scientists still commonly used these terms in the early 1900s, and most continue today as primary designations of the world's peoples.[184] However, five different races are too easy to include; therefore, we use ethnicities instead of races to deal with diversity.

---

[183] "Race (human categorization)", Encyclopedia Britannica, last accessed September 23, 2023, https://en.wikipedia.org/wiki/Race_(human_categorization)

[184] "Scientific classifications of race", Encyclopedia Britannica, last accessed September 23, 2023, https://www.britannica.com/topic/race-human/Scientific-classifications-of-race

There are more than 5,000 ethnic groups in the world.[185] Unless a corporation is a multinational operation, hires hundreds of thousands of people, and has offices, outlets, or factories worldwide. Otherwise, it is impossible to cover most ethnic groups. Therefore, diversity is localized to the city, province or country level for most corporations, institutions, and organizations. It should first cover the demographics of the local community and then extend it to the nationwide distribution.

Suppose the number of ethnic groups is fewer than the number of positions in a company. In that case, the company should try its best to ensure its employees' ethnicities cover all those groups. Of course, the existence of an ethnic group may not be significant enough to supply the required workforce. For example, a city with a population of 100,000 has 11 ethnic groups, and the smallest ethnic group has only 100 people. Among them, only 50 people are from the working class. If there are 80 companies in the city that can hire more than 20 people, not all 80 companies can hire a person from that smallest ethnic group.

As discussed in Chapter 4, equity is not absolute. Similarly, diversity is not always directly proportional to the demographics of society. For example, suppose a city has twenty ethnic groups, each representing 5% of the population.

[185] "How many major races are there in the world?", World Mysteries, last update February 18, 2011, https://blog.world-mysteries.com/science/how-many-major-races-are-there-in-the-world/

In that case, it does not mean that corporations should hire an equal number of people from each ethnic group. However, suppose the majority of employees belong to one particular ethnic group. In that case, the corporation should review its policy to ensure that its selection process is fair and complies with diversity and equity concepts. The statistics of the overall demographics of employment in that city should also be referenced.

Like equity, diversity should not be done on the surface. Some corporations and institutions hire visible minorities for positions that are easily noticed by the public, such as the receptionists at the front desk and the personnel in the public relations department, just to show that they have diversity policies. Diversity and inclusion are the tools to achieve equity; such kind of diversity done on the surface can never achieve true equity.

According to the 2016 census, the ethnic majority in Hong Kong was Han, which constituted around 92% of the population. 4.4% of the total population were foreign domestic helpers who were not permanent residents of Hong Kong.[186] Other than foreign domestic helpers, expatriates were also working in Hong Kong. However, there were no statistics on the population of minorities who were permanent residents of

---

[186] "Thematic Report : Ethnic Minorities", Census and Statistics Department of Hong Kong, last updated December 2017, https://www.censtatd.gov.hk/en/data/stat_report/product/B1120100/att/B11201002016XXXXB0100.pdf

Hong Kong. The table below shows the demographics of Hong Kong regardless of their residency status.[187]

Table 1

Ethnic group	2016 By-census	
	Number	%
Chinese	6,752,202	92.0
Filipino	184,081	2.5
Indonesian	153,299	2.1
White	58,209	0.8
Indian	36,462	0.5
Nepalese	25,472	0.3
Pakistani	18,094	0.2
Thai	10,215	0.1
Japanese	9,976	0.1
Other Asian	19,589	0.3
Others	68,986	0.9
Total	7,336,585	

As over 90% of the Hong Kong population are Chinese, they may not be sensitive enough to notice how minorities feel and understand the difficulties that minorities face. Many

---

[187] "Demographics of Hong Kong", Wikipedia, last accessed September 23, 2023, https://en.wikipedia.org/wiki/Demographics_of_Hong_Kong

Western countries, such as Canada[188] and Australia,[189] have more than 20% immigrants, and over half of them are visible minorities. As a result, those Western countries are more sensitive to minority issues and have more policies to deal with them.

Age

Ethnicities and other group types are discrete measurements, but age is a continuous measurement. People's ages change daily, from 0 to over 100, and they can be divided into different groups. A straightforward way to separate them is by using minors, working ages and retirees as the three main groups. For example, people under 18 (19 or 21, depending on the legal age in that jurisdiction) may form the first group. People aged 19 to 64 may form the second group (59 or else, depending on the retirement age in that jurisdiction), and people who are 65 and above may form the third group.

Such a simple way to classify age groups may not reflect the characteristics of different age groups. For example, the legal age to drive in some jurisdictions is 16, but the legal age to drink is 19. On the other hand, the legal age to work may be 14, gambling may be 18, and voting may be

---

[188] "Visible minority", Wikipedia, last accessed September 23, 2023, https://en.wikipedia.org/wiki/Visible_minority
[189] "Demography of Australia", Wikipedia, last accessed September 23, 2023, https://en.wikipedia.org/wiki/Demography_of_Australia

21. In that case, it is not easy to have a clear-cut division of the population into different groups by their ages. Moreover, some countries set flexible retirement ages for people to get senior benefits, making it hard to define the age of seniors.

There will be too few groups that can be used to work with diversity if we classify age into only three groups. It is like when we classify the race as five big groups; it is too easy to cover each group. Therefore, ages should be divided into intervals, such as multiples of five or ten, depending on the case. In some cases, the dividing lines for adults and seniors will still be used.

Age diversity can bring several benefits to corporations. It can promote corporate image by telling the public they care about EDI. It provides a broad spectrum to ensure its employees understand customers in different age groups, such as product designs. While young employees are generally more energetic, mature employees are more experienced. That gives a balance of actions and thoughts. Moreover, since it may take years to acquire enough experience in the field and get familiar with the operation of the company or the department, older employees may act as mentors to younger employees, especially fresh graduates. Because of their different life experience, a multigenerational workforce can have distinctive ways to analyze or perform a task and may contribute diverse skills that drive creative solutions to problems.

An ageing population is a problem in Hong Kong. In 2016, over one million people in Hong Kong were over the age of 65. It was an increase of 36.4% from 2006. The ageing trend in the population has continued, and the pace of ageing has become faster in the past decade.[190] One in five Hong Kongers aged 65 and older reported working during the year.[191] Therefore, employers, social service providers and the government may have to adjust their policies to accommodate the seniors.

Gender

As discussed above, it is easy to reflect diversity on the surface when there are only a few distinguishable groups. In the past, gender was a binary identity, having two genders, male and female. Some countries legally recognize a non-binary or third gender, including Australia, Canada and New Zealand.[192] Intersex people make up about one percent of the population.[193] The sex ratio for the world population is

[190] "Thematic Report : Older Persons", Census and Statistics Department of Hong Kong, last updated March 2018, https://www.censtatd.gov.hk/en/data/stat_report/product/B1120105/att/B11201052016XXXXB0100.pdf

[191] "Working seniors in Canada", Statistics Canada, last updated November 29, 2017, https://www12.statcan.gc.ca/census-recensement/2016/as-sa/98-200-x/2016027/98-200-x2016027-eng.cfm

[192] "Legal recognition of non-binary gender", Wikipedia, last accessed September 23, 2023, https://en.wikipedia.org/wiki/Legal_recognition_of_non-binary_gender

[193] "Intersex", Wikipedia, last accessed September 23, 2023, https://en.wikipedia.org/wiki/Intersex

estimated at 101 males to 100 females.[194] Therefore, the male and female ratio in corporations and institutions is supposed to be equal.

However, many corporations treat females the same way as visible minorities; they hire females as front desk personnel or junior staff to show diversity. A survey showed that in Fortune 500 companies, only 24 of them have females as their CEO.[195] That is an excellent example to show that diversity on the surface cannot achieve true equity, and benefits cannot be enjoyed by each group.

Diversity on the surface may also create unnecessary problems. The education provider mentioned in Chapter 4 also wanted to promote diversity by using gender-neutral names and different ethnic groups in their essays. They proposed to use Japanese and Spanish unisex names in the essays. Such diversity, on the surface, would create unnecessary problems for their students. The following is similar to one of their proposed exercises, which will confuse the learners:

> Jun married Rui, and he bought her a vintage
> bracelet from an antique store. Ariel married
> Elia, and he bought her a rose from the market.

---

[194] "Human sex ratio", Wikipedia, last accessed September 23, 2023, https://en.wikipedia.org/wiki/Human_sex_ratio

[195] "Just 24 female CEOs lead the companies on the 2018 Fortune 500—fewer than last year", CNBC, last updated May 21 2018, https://www.cnbc.com/2018/05/21/2018s-fortune-500-companies-have-just-24-female-ceos.html

1. *Who bought a bracelet?*
2. *Who bought a rose?*

The learners could not answer the questions without knowing the gender of the persons in the contents. If we write it using typical English male and female names, like most books that teach the English language, the contents and answers will be crystal clear.

> *Peter married Mary, and he bought her a vintage bracelet from an antique store. Linda married Paul, and he bought her a rose from the market.*
>
> 1. *Who bought a bracelet?*
> 2. *Who bought a rose?*
>
> *Answer 1: Peter*
> *Answer 2: Paul*

Like equity, we should not perform diversity just for political correctness on the surface but ignore the potential problems.

In politics, the first female head of state in the world was elected in Tannu Tuva[196] in 1940.[197] After that, Mongolia, India and China also elected a female head of state before

---

[196] "Tuvan People's Republic", Wikipedia, last accessed September 23, 2023, https://en.wikipedia.org/wiki/Tuvan_People%27s_Republic

[197] "List of elected and appointed female heads of state and government", Wikipedia, last accessed September 23, 2023, https://en.wikipedia.org/wiki/List_of_elected_and_appointed_female_heads_of_state_and_government

1970. However, after 80 years, the number of female politicians in all countries is low, as males still dominate the field. Of the 193 member states of the United Nations,[198] only 88 have elected female heads of state or heads of government. In the United States, there is no female elected as president yet.

Gender pay inequality is still an issue in many countries. Although research shows that female executives outearn their male peers in the United States, people are skeptical because the number of female executives included in the study is only 6% of the total sample.[199] On the other hand, reports show that the base salary of female executives was 39% lower than their male counterparts in Sweden,[200] 32% lower in Canada[201] , and 45% lower in India.[202]

---

[198] "United Nations", Wikipedia, last accessed September 23, 2023, https://en.wikipedia.org/wiki/United_Nations

[199] "Research suggests female CEOs outearn their male peers—but it's not that simple", CNBC, last updated April 10, 2018, https://www.cnbc.com/2018/04/10/research-suggests-female-ceos-outearn-men-but-its-not-that-simple.html

[200] "Is gender a factor for remuneration on CEO level? An EY analysis of the gender pay gap among CEOs of large-caps listed in Sweden", last accessed September 23, 2023, https://assets.ey.com/content/dam/ey-sites/ey-com/sv_se/news/2020/03/ey-gender-pay-gap-analysis.pdf

[201] "Even in executive ranks, women's pay is 68% of men's", The Canadian Broadcasting Corporation, last updated Jan 2, 2019, https://www.cbc.ca/news/business/ceo-pay-gender-gap-1.4963112

[202] "Glass ceiling: Pay gap between women and men CEOs doubles", The Economic Times, last updated February 8, 2020, https://economictimes.indiatimes.com/news/company/corporate-trends/glass-ceiling-pay-gap-between-women-and-men-ceos-doubles/articleshow/74019922.cms

A survey done by the Hong Kong government showed a common view that employment made women independent, but women had to sacrifice more than men to succeed. Women were still stereotyped as family carers. Discrimination against women in the workplace was still common, and women in managerial roles were being prejudiced against.[203] One of the causes for those inequalities may be that Chinese traditions are still deeply rooted. As a result, family responsibility was the primary reason that kept women from working, and women often left the workplace after giving birth.

Another cause may be that there are more women than men in Hong Kong. Its sex ratio, the comparative number of males with respect to each female in a population, was around 0.85 in 2020. It is the second-lowest ratio in the world.[204] About 54.3% of the Hong Kong population are women, which is more than four million people. However, their labour force participation rate is only 49.6%, less than the men's 66.2%. One in five mothers reported experiencing discrimination during pregnancy, maternity leave or within the first year after returning to work.[205] Other than working

[203] "What do Women and Men in Hong Kong Think about the Status of Women at Home, Work and in Social Environments?", Women's Commission of Hong Kong, last accessed September 23, 2023, https://www.women.gov.hk/download/research/WoC_Survey_Finding_Economic_E.pdf

[204] "List of countries by sex ratio", Wikipedia, last accessed September 23, 2023, https://en.wikipedia.org/wiki/List_of_countries_by_sex_ratio

[205] "Gender Equality in Hong Kong", Equal Opportunities Commission, last updated August 2021, https://www.eoc.org.hk/EOC/Upload/DiscriminationLaws/OtherResources/Gender%20Equality-Eng%20%28Aug%202021%29.pdf

mothers, more classes can be created within the female group to reflect a more diversified community, hence pinpointing and solving the problems associated with different classes.

Other Issues

Considering having a well-diversified organization is like using different KPIs (Key Performance Indicators) to evaluate the success of that organization. Each human characteristic can be a KPI if applicable. For example, people with a criminal record may be a "KPI" when assessing the employment policy of a company. However, it will not be a "KPI" for a police department, as no criminal record is a prerequisite of the hiring requirement of police. Below are some standard "KPIs" used in diversity.

<u>Creed</u>

If society has diverse religious beliefs, employers should also hire a diverse workforce in terms of religion. It is more than simply a support for the idea of diversity; but it has practical benefits.

Even small and medium-sized enterprises should be sensitive enough to deal with different religious groups in today's world. Having employees from different religious groups can help the companies know the taboos of each religion. For example, corporations can save their marketing costs and not offend anyone by not promoting food products containing pork to the Islamic, Jewish and Orthodox communities.[206] They can have first-hand information if some of their employees are religious believers.

Education and Experience

More and more employers appreciate the diversified educational background of their employees. They prefer their employees to be graduates from universities in different states or provinces, different countries, or different continents. Similarly, many employers prefer to hire people with overseas or out-of-the-province experience to give them more diversified opinions or ideas. The more considerable differences between the cultures, the more diversified experience, knowledge, and ideas contributed.

Employees with overseas education or working experience are the assets of diversity and inclusion. They can compare the policies, designs, structures or methodologies used in other countries with the local ones and make suggestions accordingly. In addition, they can be bridges among colleagues, helping others understand and accept different cultures.

An example of good practice of diversity is at Ivey Business School. It is one of the top business schools in the world and the second-largest producer and publisher of cases

---

[206] "Religious restrictions on the consumption of pork", Wikipedia, last accessed September 23, 2023, https://en.wikipedia.org/wiki/Religious_restrictions_on_the_consumptio n_of_pork

all around the world, just behind Harvard Business School.[207] It recommends that students take disciplines other than business in their first two years of study as their major subjects. The third and fourth years at Ivey will be intensive business case studies. Such a diverse learning method gives its students diversified fields of study and a broad knowledge base so that they can do their business analysis from different aspects.

Family and Marital Status

People who are single, married, have children or have no kids have different life experiences. Such experiences are helpful when dealing with customers as they will also have various backgrounds. Therefore, a team with different family and marital statuses can share their experience to deal with various customers more effectively.

Other Status

Depending on the purpose, diversity can include, but is not limited to, people with differences in the following areas:

Age
Ancestry
Career
Colour
Creed

---

[207] "Ivey Business School", Wikipedia, last accessed September 23, 2023, https://en.wikipedia.org/wiki/Ivey_Business_School

Culture
Citizenship
Education Level
Education Specialty
Family Status
Gender Identity
Language
Marital Status
Mental Disabilities
Military Experience
Overseas Experience
Physical Disabilities
Political Beliefs
Sex
Sexual Orientation
Skills
Race
Wealth

Not all of the above can be included for every function. One example is that criminal records may not be considered a positive or negative factor in accepting students to a college as a diversity approach. Political belief is a possible status on some occasions in a group to gain the benefits of diversity. For example, China allows democratic parties such as the Chinese Peasants and Workers Democratic Party,[208] China

---

[208] "Home page", Chinese Peasants and Workers Democratic Party, last accessed September 23, 2023, http://www.ngd.org.cn/

Democratic League,[209] and China Democracy Promotion Association[210] to exist and operate. Although they have to be under the leadership of the Chinese Communist Party, such an arrangement allows the government, or the Chinese Communist Party, to have different angles to review their policies.

[209] "Home page", China Democratic League, last accessed September 23, 2023, http://www.dem-league.org.cn/
[210] "Home page", China Democracy Promotion Association, last accessed September 23, 2023https://www.mj.org.cn/

6. Inclusion

Inclusion refers to creating an environment where everyone feels welcome and respected, especially those with historical disadvantages, such as females, older adults, and persons with disabilities. Inclusion can provide an atmosphere where everyone can fully participate in the organization without hindrance.

Some people applied inclusion to only persons with disabilities[211] or only in education,[212] especially during the initial period when the concept of EDI was introduced. Inclusion should be diverse enough to include all classes of people, regardless of their gender, age, disability, creed, ethnic background, marital status, family status, and other grounds that can be subject to discrimination. While inclusion is diverse, a diverse group is not always inclusive. A diverse community can just be a community that consists of different groups of people, but people may still treat each other unfairly. An inclusive environment provides equity and respect to all types of people, and it accepts and values differences of diversity. Simply put, inclusion is accepting all kinds of people without discrimination.

---

[211] "Inclusion (disability rights)", Wikipedia, last accessed September 23, 2023, https://en.wikipedia.org/wiki/Inclusion_(disability_rights)

[212] "Inclusion (education)", Wikipedia, last accessed September 23, 2023, https://en.wikipedia.org/wiki/Inclusion_(education)

Empathy

To have a thriving, inclusive culture, people must understand what others are experiencing within their culture, religion, age, gender, and other traits that may cause discrimination or inequality. That is, they must have enough empathy to get along with others. If they are the policymakers, they must have the empathy to set out suitable policies for applying inclusion.

Since the outbreak of COVID-19, most white collars have been required to work from home. People use online tools for meetings and presentations. A report showed that the majority would want to keep working from home even after the pandemic if they had a choice.[213] Such a change in work mode made many executives study the possibility of working remotely after the pandemic. Some of them had already changed their policies to allow employees to work remotely permanently.[214] That would save the employees time commuting and the office rental costs for the corporations. Many employees could also move to suburban areas to avoid

---

[213] "How the Coronavirus Outbreak Has – and Hasn't – Changed the Way Americans Work", Pew Research Center, last updated Decemeber 9, 2020, https://www.pewresearch.org/social-trends/2020/12/09/how-the-coronavirus-outbreak-has-and-hasnt-changed-the-way-americans-work/

[214] "Covid Is Forcing Video Game Companies to Rethink Remote Work", Bloomberg, last updated October 15, 2021, https://www.bloomberg.com/news/articles/2021-10-15/covid-forces-video-game-makers-to-rethink-remote-work

the high rental rates in the big cities when they work from home.[215]

The working time is another example. One hundred years ago, a six-day workweek was the cultural norm. It was reduced to today's five-day workweek because of the advocacy of the unions.[216] Some corporations have begun offering their employees a four-day workweek to accommodate the demand for better work-life balance.[217] Two towns, one in Nova Scotia and one in Ontario, also tested a four-day workweek, and both turned out very successful.[218]

As more and more people are looking for flexible work arrangements to take care of their families, many companies also offer flexible working hours to their employees. Many employees can choose their work hours between 7 a.m. and 7 p.m. as long as the core hours (between 11 a.m. and 3 p.m.) are covered.[219] Although the norm in the world is eight

---

[215] "Amazon will allow many employees to work remotely, indefinitely. Affected businesses react", The Seattle Times, last updated October 12, 2021, https://www.seattletimes.com/business/amazon/amazon-will-allow-many-employees-to-work-remotely-indefinitely/

[216] "Four-day workweek", Wikipedia, last accessed September 23, 2023, https://en.wikipedia.org/wiki/Four-day_workweek

[217] "Ontario CEO tests four-day work week for employees, says she won't go back", City News, last updated October 13,2021, https://toronto.ctvnews.ca/ontario-ceo-tests-four-day-work-week-for-employees-says-she-won-t-go-back-1.5621892

[218] "A 4-Day Workweek Was Tested In This Small Canadian Town & Here's What Happened Next", Narcity, last updated October 14, 2021, https://www.narcity.com/a-4-day-workweek-was-tested-in-a-nova-scotia-town-the-morale-boost-made-it-all-worth-it

[219] "Flextime", Wikipedia, last accessed September 23, 2023, https://en.wikipedia.org/wiki/Flextime

working hours per day,[220] many corporations in Canada and the US offer a 35-hour workweek. A 35-hour workweek is just a benefit offered by companies in North America, but it is a law in France.[221]

Because of the four-day workweek, some employers reduced the number of working hours per week to thirty-two; some even reduced it to twenty-eight hours.[222] However, some of them maintain the total weekly hours at 35 but with four 8.75-hour days instead of five 7-hour days. Therefore, although a four-day workweek may become the norm, it may not fit all types of businesses, such as hourly paid work and jobs requiring intense concentration. For example, the productivity of computer programming may drop with longer shifts. Nevertheless, cutting the working hours per week is an inclusive decision that shows empathy to people who need more time to spend with their families, such as small kids or relatives with terminal illnesses, or simply for a better work-life balance.

Reducing the working hours per day and working days per week is a result of inclusion. Employers understand that many employees need to take care of their young kids, spend more time with their families, or simply have a better life-work

---

[220] "Working time", Wikipedia, last accessed September 23, 2023, https://en.wikipedia.org/wiki/Working_time

[221] "35-hour workweek", Wikipedia, last accessed September 23, 2023, https://en.wikipedia.org/wiki/35-hour_workweek

[222] "Germany's 28-Hour Workweek", Jacobin, last updated March 24, 2018, https://www.jacobinmag.com/2018/03/germanys-28-hour-workweek

balance to improve their mental health. Changing the work time is only one of the issues that need empathy. Without empathy, employers might take longer to understand the needs of their employees and might not provide better employment benefits to retain good employees.

Respect

Respecting other groups is the first step in an inclusive culture. It is crucial to respect others by understanding that different people have different characteristics, such as male versus female, youth versus older adults, and Western versus Eastern culture. It is also essential to allow other people to have their own choices, such as sexual orientation, family status, or religious beliefs.

The changing rooms in gymnasiums and swimming pools used to be open-style. People changed their clothes and took showers in an open area. Shower stalls were installed later to provide better privacy, but most were without doors or curtains. Many places offer separate changing and shower rooms with doors or curtains to respect people's privacy. That is exceptionally important for people with gender identity issues, and such arrangements show respect to them.

Many public bathrooms have improved stalls for persons with disabilities. The stalls are more significant than the ordinary stalls to provide space for wheelchair access. In addition, they have rails to help persons with disabilities to support their bodies or keep balance. The water faucets are specially designed so that persons with disabilities can pull the handle to activate water flow without using much force. The new technology even makes some of them touchless. The sinks are also mounted high enough with clear floor space underneath to allow wheelchair access.

Those unique features show respect for and inclusion of persons with disabilities. However, they can be further improved. All sinks and faucets in public washrooms can be the same type so that persons with disabilities will not feel they are different and need special care. If space is not an issue, the size of all stalls should also be big enough for wheelchair access. If that cannot be done, at least all stalls should have rails because they can also provide assistance to older adults.

Institutions and corporations may have their dress code, such as wearing a uniform, a hat or a helmet. Some religious believers, such as Sikhs and Islamics, may have to wear a turban that is too thick to fit into a hat or a helmet. As a result, they would seek exemptions. While some industries rejected the idea for safety reasons,[223] some are ordered by the courts to allow the practice of wearing turbans instead of

---

[223] "No hard hat, no deal: Quebec court becomes latest to slap down turban exemptions for Sikhs", National Post, last updated September 29, 2016, https://nationalpost.com/news/canada/no-hard-hat-no-deal-quebec-court-becomes-latest-to-slap-down-turban-exemptions-for-sikhs

hats or helmets.[224] Employers should proactively look for alternatives to allow their employees to practice their religious beliefs without limitations set by their dress code.

Acceptance

Accepting another culture, religion, or group does not mean we have to be the same. Accepting other groups means acknowledging them and allowing them to live, behave, or believe what they want, but not transforming yourself into one. That is unnecessary and sometimes impossible.

For example, suppose you are a white male; accepting a black female does not mean changing yourself into a black female. Similarly, heterosexual people who accept the LGBT group do not have to participate or become members of the LGBT group. Instead, true inclusion is treating the LGBT group like everyone else — ordinary and nothing special except providing assistance when needed.

Acceptance includes the recognition and allowance of doing things differently. Sometimes, authorities are too rigid to allow people to have their own approaches to solving problems, even if their solutions are better than those

---

[224] "The turban that rocked the RCMP: How Baltej Singh Dhillon challenged the RCMP — and won", The Canadian Broadcasting Corporation, last update May 11, 2017, https://www.cbc.ca/2017/canadathestoryofus/the-turban-that-rocked-the-rcmp-how-baltej-singh-dhillon-challenged-the-rcmp-and-won-1.4110271

recommended by the authorities. Because of COVID-19, a school board in Ontario required all their teachers to wear masks provided by the board. Instead of wearing the mask provided by the board, a teacher who wanted an extra layer of protection wore an N95 mask. N95 masks are more protective than the medical masks provided by the board. However, the teacher was threatened with disciplinary action for wearing it.[225]

That is a counterexample of inclusion. The school board should have accepted the "better equipment" used by the teacher. An epidemiologist said the masks issued by the board were "low quality" and "inadequate". To draw an analogy, the rule to wear a mask provided by the board is like a rule requiring the teachers to dress appropriately, such as no vast and shorts. Wearing an N95 mask is like wearing a long-sleeved shirt and long pants. The reaction of the school board was too much and definitely not inclusive.

EDI is constantly promoted by politicians, which is good for society. However, sometimes, they just focus on the surface and make it politically correct instead of setting a real EDI environment. For example, in Western countries, especially within governments and big corporations, people stopped using the term "*Merry Christmas*" to send greetings at Christmas. They now use "*Happy Holidays*" instead.

---

[225] "York Region teachers reportedly threatened with disciplinary action for wearing N95 masks", City News, last updated October 13, 2021, https://toronto.citynews.ca/2021/10/13/york-region-district-school-board-n95-masks/

Accepting other religions does not mean we have to restrain one particular religion, regardless of the target.

Restricting saying or writing *"Merry Christmas"* is a negative approach to promoting inclusion or equity. A positive and proactive approach encourages the acceptance of other religions, cultures or orientations. We can say *"Shabbat Shalom"* (meaning Good Sabbath) to non-Jewish people, *"Eid Mubarak"* (meaning Happy Eid) to non-Islam people, and *"Shubh Diwali"* (meaning Happy Diwali) to non-Hindu people. It is something like the Google Doodle,[226] and no one shall feel offended, although the greetings and blessings may not apply to them. Similarly, we can also promote different cultural festivals according to the demographic distribution in the city or country, such as Rosh Hashanah, Dragon Boat Festival and Dia De Los Muertos.

The concept of inclusion is similar to the idea of living in a global village, where everyone belongs to the same society that coexists through transnational commerce, migration, and culture.[227] When everyone is a resident of the same *"village"*, we should acknowledge and accept the existence of different cultures, beliefs and characteristics of other groups of people.

---

[226] "Google Doodle", Wikipedia, last accessed September 23, 2023, https://en.wikipedia.org/wiki/Google_Doodle
[227] "Global village", Wikipedia, last accessed September 23, 2023, https://en.wikipedia.org/wiki/Global_village

Inclusion should be promoted as treating others like your family and friends by putting yourself in other people's shoes. For example, suppose there are Jewish, Islamic and Buddhist employees in a corporation. In that case, the management can designate a special refrigerator to keep Kosher[228] food items separate from other foods, porks separate from other things, and meats separate from vegetable items.

Many corporations have already had the policy to provide flexible working hours to their employees if they need to pray or worship their gods during working hours. Such a policy to accommodate the employees' needs is also a kind of inclusion by showing that it is acceptable to excuse them from work temporarily because of their religious beliefs. In some jurisdictions, it is against the law if an employer does not provide accommodations to employees to practice their religion or not to do it in a respectful manner.[229]

We must accept that different cultures have divergent meanings for the same thing. One billion was commonly referred to as 1,000,000,000,000 in the United Kingdom in the past. Now, it means 1,000,000,000. Football means soccer in most countries, the ball game that is played by kicking the ball to score a goal. In North America, football means the game

---

[228] "Kosher foods", Wikipedia, last accessed September 23, 2023, https://en.wikipedia.org/wiki/Kosher_foods

[229] "The duty to accommodate", Ontario Human Rights Commission, last accessed September 23, 2023, http://www.ohrc.on.ca/en/policy-preventing-discrimination-based-creed/9-duty-accommodate

evolved from rugby. Different cultures may also have their unique body language and gestures. In India, a head bobble does not mean disagreement or no. Depending on the context, it may mean yes, good, maybe, okay, or I understand.[230] Understanding and accepting different cultures can improve inclusion in society.

Value

We must value the contributions that different groups can bring to corporations, institutions and societies. Each employee or citizen can contribute their talents to the corporation or organization regardless of their race, physical strength, age, sex or education level. Employers and governments should show appreciation and respect to all groups of people for their different values and acknowledge their contributions. They may encourage others by simply saying some kind words, showing their support by just showing up at an event, or helping a charity by volunteering their time or donating their money.

A diverse group can improve the outcome if an organization needs talents for creativity. Diversity can increase creativity in a group because it has different backgrounds – education, age, culture, life experience and more. Since over 99% of new inventions and ideas are based

---

[230] "Head booble", Wikipedia, last accessed September 23, 2023, https://en.wikipedia.org/wiki/Head_bobble

on existing facts or concepts,[231] a diverse group knows more facts and concepts than a unitary group; thus, it can contribute more ideas. Naturally, they can exchange their experience and cultural differences to explore new approaches that are unknown to a monotype group of people.

There are more than 100 different languages used in Europe[232] and 24 official languages in the European Union.[233] European governments know the importance of language skills. Therefore, they promoted multilingualism and suggested that at least two foreign languages be taught to all pupils from an early age.[234]

In a diverse Europe, students know the importance of multilingualism and employees are expected to know more than one language. In fact, proficiency in English is associated with a higher probability of being employed in Cyprus, Spain, and Finland. People who know at least some French are more likely to be employed in Malta. Those who know German are more likely to be employed in Denmark, and Russian is

[231] Bryan Law, *Differential Cogitation* (Toronto: Fox College of Business, 2020), 5

[232] "Languages of Europe", Wikipedia, last accessed September 23, 2023, https://en.wikipedia.org/wiki/Languages_of_Europe

[233] "EU languages", European Union, last accessed September 23, 2023, https://europa.eu/european-union/about-eu/eu-languages_en

[234] "Foreign language learning statistics", Statistics Explained, last updated, February 22, 2021, https://ec.europa.eu/eurostat/statistics-explained/index.php?title=Foreign_language_learning_statistics

associated with a higher probability of being employed in Bulgaria, Latvia, Lithuania, and Poland.[235]

Using the European experience, employers in other countries should value their employees who know more than one language. Likewise, job seekers should be proud of their multicultural background and multilingualism, which can bring value to their employers.

In order to let employees with different backgrounds contribute their value in a stressless and comfortable environment, employers should accommodate their needs whenever possible. Sometimes, those accommodations may also fit other employees' needs or provide convenience to them. For example, corporations may give big-screen monitors for employees to use with their notebooks or PCs. This valuable tool is not only for older adults with presbyopia but also makes using computers more comfortable for all employees.

Providing transgender washrooms is another area to show the inclusion culture and appreciation of the value brought by transgender people. Some organizations provide individual washrooms that fit all genders, so they do not have to be afraid to enter a "special washroom" and be recognized or labelled as "special".

---

[235] Michele Gazzola and Daniele Mazzacani, *Foreign language skills and employment status of European natives: evidence from Germany, Italy and Spain.* (Empirica 46, 2019), 713–740.

Equity

Without inclusion, we cannot achieve equity. It was common for the people of two villages to have quarrels, fights, and even wars in ancient times. Those villagers lived in the same country, belonged to the same ethnic group, and shared culture and language. One could not tell the difference between them unless they told you where they lived. Most of their fight was because they refused to share resources with another village or simply felt that they were better than the other villagers.

When one group of people feels superior to the others and refuses to accept that other groups have the same quality as they have, it is easy to generate discrimination. In the age of black slavery, some people even rationalized their discrimination with pseudoscientific ideas to conclude that black people were inferior to white people. They started with physical and intellectual inferiority theories that likened blacks to animals, especially monkeys and apes.[236] That evolved to black social inferiority and systematic discrimination as the final result.

---

[236] "A brief history of the enduring phony science that perpetuates white supremacy", The Washington Post, last updated April 30, 2019, https://www.washingtonpost.com/local/a-brief-history-of-the-enduring-phony-science-that-perpetuates-white-supremacy/2019/04/29/20e6aef0-5aeb-11e9-a00e-050dc7b82693_story.html

Similarly, the Japanese believed they were superior to other ethnic groups, except the Germans.[237] During World War II, the Imperial Japanese Army treated the people of other countries as animals and slaughtered more than ten million civilians.[238] Just in Nanjing, a city in China, more than 300,000 civilians were murdered over six weeks.[239] The Imperial Japanese Army even had a contest to behead Chinese civilians using a sword.[240] The feeling of superiority was the cause of all those inhumane behaviours, as they thought they had the right to treat other people like animals. We must accept that all ethnic groups are equal and treat everyone equally.

Promoting inclusion and diversity is the process of achieving the ultimate goal – equity. The points system to approach equity will be discussed in Chapter 7, while how inclusion will affect equity will be addressed in this section. To use inclusion to achieve equity, we should not overdo it. For example, one should not discriminate against the LGBT group, but it does not mean that the heterosexual group has

---

[237] "Japan Times 1971: Japanese believe they are 'superior'", The Japan Times, last updated June 6, 2021, https://www.japantimes.co.jp/news/2021/06/06/national/history/japan-times-gone-by-1971/

[238] "Japanese war crimes", Wikipedia, last accessed September 23, 2023, https://en.wikipedia.org/wiki/Japanese_war_crimes

[239] "Nanjing Massacre", Wikipedia, last accessed September 23, 2023, https://en.wikipedia.org/wiki/Nanjing_Massacre

[240] "Contest to kill 100 people using a sword", Wikipedia, last accessed September 23, 2023, https://en.wikipedia.org/wiki/Contest_to_kill_100_people_using_a_sword

to promote the LGBT group or vice versa. Both the LGBT group and heterosexual group should respect each other and treat each other fairly. Like political orientation, sexual orientation is a personal choice, and everyone should respect other people's choices. Forcing one group of people to promote another group may be offensive. The concept and feeling can be easily understood when the subject matter is religion.

Some ethnic groups believe their cultures, religions, and languages are superior to other ethnic groups, especially the Indigenous people. That was why Canada established boarding schools to assimilate Indigenous children and youth into Western culture. Christian missionaries were also involved. The first school was founded in 1834, and the last one was closed in 1996. Around 150,000 Indigenous children were placed in residential schools nationally during that period of time.[241]

Students were placed there without proper health care, and as a result, many of them died at the schools. More than 3,000 Indigenous children and youth died in residential schools on record, and those who had the power to prevent these deaths did little to stop them.[242] The remains of

---

[241] "Canadian Indian residential school system", Wikipedia, last accessed September 23, 2023, https://en.wikipedia.org/wiki/Canadian_Indian_residential_school_syst em

[242] "Truth and Reconciliation Commission's report details deaths of 3,201 children in residential schools", Toronto Star, last updated December 15, 2015, https://www.thestar.com/news/canada/2015/12/15/truth-and-

children[243] and unmarked graves[244] were buried at former residential schools[245] on and off.[246] The appointed Truth and Reconciliation Commission even called that cultural genocide.[247] The number of school-related deaths remains unknown due to incomplete records, but it may keep rising.[248]

The United States had similar boarding schools during the early 19th and mid-20th centuries, and Christian churches were also involved. Those schools were often overcrowded, and there was a lack of public sanitation. As a result, the students were at risk for infectious diseases such as

reconciliation-commissions-report-details-deaths-of-3201-children-in-residential-schools.html

[243] "Remains of 215 children found buried at former B.C. residential school, First Nation says", The Canadian Broadcasting Corporation, last updated May 29, 2021, https://www.cbc.ca/news/canada/british-columbia/tk-eml%C3%BAps-te-secw%C3%A9pemc-215-children-former-kamloops-indian-residential-school-1.6043778

[244] "Canada: 751 unmarked graves found at residential school", The British Broadcasting Corporation, last updated June 2, 2021, https://www.bbc.com/news/world-us-canada-57592243

[245] "From truth to reconciliation: How to move forward with the TRC's calls to action", Global News, last updated June 26, 2021, https://globalnews.ca/news/7982370/truth-reconciliation-how-to-move-forward-residential-schools/

[246] "More unmarked graves discovered in British Columbia at a former indigenous residential school known as 'Canada's Alcatraz'", The Cable News Network, last updated July 13, 2021, https://www.cnn.com/2021/07/13/americas/canada-unmarked-indigenous-graves/index.html

[247] "Truth and Reconciliation Commission", The Canadian Encyclopedia, last updated September 24, 2015, https://www.thecanadianencyclopedia.ca/en/article/truth-and-reconciliation-commission

[248] "More graves are found at Canadian schools for the indigenous", The Econimist, last updated July 3, 2021, https://www.economist.com/the-americas/2021/07/03/more-graves-are-found-at-canadian-schools-for-the-indigenous

tuberculosis, measles and trachoma.[249] Thousands of children have died in these schools through beatings, medical neglect and malnutrition. One scholar estimated that 40,000 children might have been killed in or because of their poor care at those schools.[250]

In Australia, its government even passed laws to remove Indigenous children from their families and placed them in institutional facilities operated by religious or charitable organizations during the late 19th and early 20th centuries.[251] All those boarding schools and removals of Indigenous children from their families resulted from racism that must be eliminated and not happen again.

How to deliver equity without sacrificing true inclusion is a challenging issue. It is because true inclusion should include the people who provide equity and inclusion, who sometimes are the victims of discrimination for that reason. Take abortion as an example. In many jurisdictions, abortion is legal.[252] Therefore, medical practitioners must assist patients with abortion if their requests fulfill the legal

---

[249] "American Indian boarding schools", Wikipedia, last accessed September 23, 2023, https://en.wikipedia.org/wiki/American_Indian_boarding_schools

[250] "Native Americans decry unmarked graves, untold history of boarding schools", Reuters, last updated June 22, 2021, https://www.reuters.com/world/us/native-americans-decry-unmarked-graves-untold-history-boarding-schools-2021-06-22/

[251] "Stolen Generations", Wikipedia, last accessed September 23, 2023, https://en.wikipedia.org/wiki/Stolen_Generations

[252] "Abortion law", Wikipedia, last accessed September 23, 2023, https://en.wikipedia.org/wiki/Abortion_law

requirements. However, abortion may violate the religious beliefs of some practitioners. The compromised solution is that those doctors who object on moral grounds to providing abortion services to their patients must offer them a referral to another doctor. That rule also applies to services such as assisted dying and birth control.[253] Moreover, the acts of violence committed against individuals and organizations that perform abortions or provide abortion counselling are almost nonstop and should be condemned.[254]

Sometimes, the practice of inclusion and equity can be controversial issues. For example, allowing transgender people to participate in competitive sports may cause unfairness to other people.[255] Although the International Olympic Committee has a policy to require the testosterone levels of transgender athletes to be below ten nanomoles per litre for at least 12 months prior to the competition, such a requirement still cannot 100% ensure that transgender athletes have no unfair advantage over female competitors.[256] For example, males are 7% taller than females on average,[257]

---

253 "Ontario's top court rules religious doctors must offer patients an 'effective referral' for assisted dying, abortion", The Globe and Mail, last updated May 15, 2019, https://www.theglobeandmail.com/canada/article-religious-doctors-must-make-referrals-for-assisted-dying-abortion/
254 "Anti-abortion violence", Wikipedia, last accessed September 23, 2023, https://en.wikipedia.org/wiki/Anti-abortion_violence
255 "Transgender people in sports", Wikipedia, last accessed September 23, 2023, https://en.wikipedia.org/wiki/Transgender_people_in_sports
256 "Sex verification in sports", Wikipedia, last accessed September 23, 2023, https://en.wikipedia.org/wiki/Sex_verification_in_sports
257 "Human Height", Our World In Data, last updated May, 2019 https://ourworldindata.org/human-height

and males have a larger skeletal size and bone mass than females for the comparable body size.[258] Those characteristics will not be changed after gender transformation and may give unfair advantages to transexual female athletes. On the other hand, some women may produce a high level of natural testosterone that violates the rules on the hormone and are barred from the events.[259]

Organizing the Gay Games[260] shows the inclusive intention, but that is only on the surface and is not true inclusion. Although the intention is to promote the inclusion of the LGBT group, Gay Games is like racial segregation; it separates athletes into two groups – the LGBT group and the non-LGBT group. The ultimate effect may not be a good promotion of inclusion but the opposite. True inclusion should encourage the LGBT group to participate in the Summer and Winter Olympics like all other athletes and not treat them as special people who need special sports games that exclude other athletes.

---

[258] "Males Have Larger Skeletal Size and Bone Mass Than Females, Despite Comparable Body Size", American Society for Bone and Mineral Research, last updated December 4, 2009, https://asbmr.onlinelibrary.wiley.com/doi/full/10.1359/JBMR.041005

[259] "Rules governing Olympic runners send a disturbing message to female athletes, especially those who are Black", The Canadian Broadcasting Corporation, last updated July 7, 2021, https://www.cbc.ca/sports/opinion-case-of-namibian-runners-further-exposes-half-baked-testosterone-regulation-1.6092033

[260] "Gay Games", Wikipedia, last accessed September 23, 2023, https://en.wikipedia.org/wiki/Gay_Games

Finally, we must admit that educating people to understand the importance of inclusion and achieving true inclusion and equity takes time. For example, in 2001, the first Muslim female firefighter was allowed to wear the hijab on duty in the United States.[261] The first one allowed in Canada was in 2019,[262] and in the United Kingdom, it was in 2021.[263]

Inclusion is a process of respecting, accepting and valuing other people, regardless of their characteristics. A good inclusion concept is always considering other people by putting yourself in their shoes. For example, an online registration site should accommodate visually impaired people using audio input and output features. In some countries, there are still people with illiteracy, and they may also get the benefits of such a feature.

The two main steps in inclusion are empathy and reconciliation. We must understand the difficulties that every group of people faces, share their feelings, and do something to support them. If an organization or a government makes a mistake, it should be remedied. Many governments made

---

[261] "Female Muslim Firefighter Allowed to Wear Headscarf", The President and Fellows of Harvard College, last updated July 12, 2001, https://hwpi.harvard.edu/pluralismarchive/news/female-muslim-firefighter-allowed-wear-headscarf-0

[262] "Canada's first Hijabi firefighter", City News, last updated April 29, 2019, https://edmonton.citynews.ca/video/2019/04/29/canadas-first-hijabi-firefighter/

[263] "Britain's first hijab-wearing firefighter urges other Muslim women to follow her", The Mirror, last updated April 27, 2021, https://www.mirror.co.uk/news/uk-news/britains-first-hijab-wearing-firefighter-23993262

policies to show their efforts in fighting discrimination or making up for mistakes. Although most do not involve apology or compensation, their actions are the first step toward reconciliation.

Due to the impact of the Black Lives Matter movement, the City of Toronto decided to rename its "Dundas Street", a street named after Henry Dundas.[264] It is because Henry Dundas, an 18th-century British politician, delayed the abolition of slavery in Britain by 15 years. More than one hundred names have been changed in the United States and the United Kingdom[265] due to the George Floyd protests.[266] That also includes some common words in our daily lives, such as the "primary bedroom". Now, it is called the "main bedroom" or "primary bedroom".

On July 6, 2021, Canada appointed its first Indigenous governor general after human remains and unmarked graves were found at different sites of former residential schools.[267]

---

[264] "Toronto city council approves renaming Dundas Street due to namesake's connection to slavery", Global News, last updated July 14, 2021, https://globalnews.ca/news/8028570/toronto-city-council-dundas-street-renaming/

[265] "List of name changes due to the George Floyd protests", Wikipedia, last accessed September 23, 2023, https://en.wikipedia.org/wiki/List_of_name_changes_due_to_the_George_Floyd_protests

[266] "George_Floyd_protests", Wikipedia, last accessed September 23, 2023, https://en.wikipedia.org/wiki/George_Floyd_protests

[267] "Prime Minister announces The Queen's approval of Canada's next Governor General", Office of the Prime Minister (Canada), last updated July 6, 2021, https://pm.gc.ca/en/news/news-releases/2021/07/06/prime-minister-announces-queens-approval-canadas-next-governor

The appointment came as a sign of reconciliation after more unmarked graves were discovered on former residential school grounds across Canada. The appointment is praised by many people, including a grand chief of the Indigenous people, as a meaningful reconciliation between colonial governments and Indigenous people.[268]

[268] "Canada's first indigenous governor general pledges to help heal nation", The Reuters, last updated July 6, 2021, https://www.reuters.com/world/canadas-first-indigenous-governor-general-pledges-help-heal-nation-2021-07-06/

7. A Points System

Statistics

We must rely on statistics to assess the situations disadvantaged groups face, such as their population and participation ratios. However, statistics can be manipulated and used to mislead people. For example, we assume that the most comfortable water temperature to take a bath or soak feet is 40°C. A survey is then conducted whereby participants vote to feel comfortable or not by putting their feet into two buckets of water – one at 10°C and the other at 70°C. Although the average temperature of the two buckets is 40°C, participants are sure to respond that it would not be comfortable. This example highlights one way in which statistical results can be misleading – using the average.

All data used in assessing the situation should be the official statistics from the governments, their agencies or other reliable sources. For example, demographic data such as ethnic population and age distribution can be found in the national census. Raw data is the best format for statistical analysis. However, consolidating each of them consumes the most significant amount of time.

For example, a survey is done to study the age, height and weight of a group of people. Each person fills in the information so that each data will have all three numbers of that person. Analysts will have to consolidate the individual data and extract the information they need. They can generate information such as the average age or the average height of the group. They can also divide the number of people in the group using age, height or weight, such as 5,000 people in the group are younger than 65 and 1,000 people are 65 and above. However, the users who get this piece of information alone may not know other details, such as the average height of the people, unless the analysts want to share the information.

For example, if we are only given the average age of the group, we cannot find out how many people are younger than 65 and how many are 65 or older. Conversely, if we only know the number of people younger than 65 and those who are 65 or older, we cannot calculate the average age of the group. Therefore, we should gather as much information as possible, and only the raw data can give the flexibility to study statistics thoroughly.

An excellent system to achieve equity relies on demographics, education, welfare and more statistics. For example, only 4.9% of the population of Canada were Indigenous people in 2020,[269] but they represented more than 30% of inmates in Canadian prisons.[270] In the United States,

---

[269] "Annual Report to Parliament 2020", Government of Canada, last updated November 3, 2020, https://www.sac-isc.gc.ca/eng/1602010609492/1602010631711

[270] "'National travesty': report shows one third of Canada's prisoners are Indigenous", The Guardian News, last updated January 22, 2020, https://www.theguardian.com/world/2020/jan/22/one-third-canada-prisoners-indigenous-report

only 13.4% of the population were black people,[271] but they represented 33% of the prisoners in 2020.[272] Although this number had declined from 40% in 2010,[273] it was still an extremely high ratio compared to its total population.

The two examples above show that there are problems in the Indigenous communities in Canada and the black communities in the United States. Fair chances to education, employment, housing and welfare may be the solution but may not be the only ones. Moreover, a fair chance may not be the complete solution because those disadvantaged groups may need a boost, not just a fair chance, to improve their current situations.

An objective assessment of the situations and a fair system to assist them are required to achieve equity among all groups of people. For example, we must know the reasons that caused the high ratio of Indigenous and black people in the prisons, which may be lack of education, systematic discrimination by other groups or other reasons. Suppose lack of education is one of the causes. In that case, providing a living allowance for Indigenous and black people to go to

[271] "Quick Facts", United States Census Bureau, last accessed September 23, 2023, https://www.census.gov/quickfacts/fact/table/US/PST045219
[272] "Black imprisonment rate in the U.S. has fallen by a third since 2006", Pew Research Center, last updated May 6, 2020, https://www.pewresearch.org/fact-tank/2020/05/06/share-of-black-white-hispanic-americans-in-prison-2018-vs-2006/
[273] "Incarceration in the United States", Wikipedia, last accessed September 23, 2023, https://en.wikipedia.org/wiki/Incarceration_in_the_United_States

school or vocational college may help them find jobs and improve their quality of life, which may indirectly reduce their percentage of prisoners.

Similarly, the African-American unemployment rate has consistently doubled the white unemployment rate in the last 50 years.[274] The unemployment rates of Asian and Hispanic Americans are also significantly higher than that of white Americans.[275] We need to know the causes of the gaps. We cannot change the prisoner rates by setting different thresholds for conviction according to the ethnic group, which is injustice. However, we can change the unemployment rates by placing different selection criteria to help minorities get employed.

The situations in Canada are similar to those in the US. In July 2020, the unemployment rate of South Asian Canadians was 17.8%, Arab Canadians was 17.3%, and Black Canadians was 16.8%. The national unemployment rate was only 9.3% for those who did not identify as "visible minority" or "Aboriginal".[276]

---

[274] "On the Persistence of the Black-White Unemployment Gap", Center for American Progress, last updated February 24, 2020, https://www.americanprogress.org/issues/economy/reports/2020/02/24/480743/persistence-black-white-unemployment-gap/

[275] "Unemployment rates by age, sex, race, and Hispanic or Latino ethnicity", U.S. Bureau of Labor Statistics, last updated July 02, 2021, https://www.bls.gov/web/empsit/cpsee_e16.htm

[276] "New race-based unemployment data show higher rates for Black, Arab and South Asian Canadians" CBC, last updated August 7, 2020, https://www.cbc.ca/news/canada/british-columbia/race-based-unemployment-data-pandemic-1.5679127

On the other hand, there is no significant difference in the unemployment rates of immigrants and citizens born in Canada, regardless of the time they settled in Canada.[277] The finding indicates that local education and experience are not the main factors affecting the employment rate, but ethnicity is. To achieve equity, we want a diversified labour force so that the unemployment rates are the same among different groups (not just ethnic groups). Inclusion will provide a comfortable environment for the employees.

A Fair System

As we need to boost the disadvantaged groups, a fair system is required to give them merits to gain advantages and compensate for their situations. The term "fair" is crucial and should apply to everyone and society as a whole, not just to disadvantaged groups.

Take the previous example; when the number of Indigenous and black prisoners is significantly higher than that of other ethnic groups, we want to lower the number. However, no one will agree that we should raise the threshold for prosecuting Indigenous and black suspects to reduce the chance of successful prosecution. However, if we do it that way, the number of Indigenous and black prisoners will

---

[277] "Labour force characteristics by immigrant status, annual", Statistics Canada, last updated January 26, 2021, https://www150.statcan.gc.ca/t1/tbl1/en/tv.action?pid=1410008301

definitely be reduced; such an approach is unfair to other people and is unjust in principle.

In 2014, California passed a law called *The Safe Neighborhoods and Schools Act*,[278] which categorizes some nonviolent offences, such as shoplifting for the value of property stolen not exceeding $950, as misdemeanours rather than felonies. It was said that the Act had reduced the state's prison population by 13,000.[279] Suppose a state in the US passes such a law but limits it to only Indigenous and black people. In that case, the number of Indigenous and black prisoners in that state will be reduced. However, that is clearly not a fair approach to solving the problem because having two types of laws for different ethnic people is unjust. Moreover, such a law may only solve the problem of the high prison population but not the fundamental issues of crimes and poverty.

A similar situation happens in education, but it is the opposite — it is believed that too many people of a minority group benefit from the system. Some people blame top universities and medical schools for accepting too many Asian students. As a result, they want to reduce the number of Asian students in those universities and schools. One of the methods is to raise the requirements of acceptance of Asian

---

[278] "Proposition 47: The Safe Neighborhoods and Schools Act", Judicial Council of California, last accessed September 23, 2023, https://www.courts.ca.gov/prop47.htm

[279] "2014 California Proposition 47", Wikipedia, last accessed September 23, 2023, https://en.wikipedia.org/wiki/2014_California_Proposition_47

students. That is why some said Asian students need much higher SAT scores than white, Hispanic and black students to enter famous private universities.

Every university has its minimum academic admission requirement of accepting students according to different programs. Raising or lowering such requirements to limit or allow a particular ethnic group of students to study at the university is an unfair policy. Students who fulfill the minimum academic admission requirements should be granted the same academic qualification regardless of their background. Disadvantaged groups may be assessed and given additional merits, but such merits should not be mixed with their academic achievements so that the minimum admission requirement will not be compromised. That is exceptionally important for professional degrees such as medical doctors, as no one wants incompetent students to become doctors just because of their ethnicity or other reasons.

For example, suppose a medical school requires students to have an SAT score of 1,400 as the minimum admission requirement. In that case, the school should not lower such a requirement for any reason, such as ethnicity or age. Lowering the academic requirement brings no benefit to the medical school, the students and society. The students who are based on a lower score get accepted may have difficulties studying, as they are not prepared for such high-level learning. The medical school will have difficulty maintaining its reputation due to the incapabilities of some of those students.

Some said those incompetent students would not be able to graduate, so the public is protected from having incompetent doctors. However, the chance is that some talented students may not be admitted to medical school because the limited spots have been awarded to those students who enjoyed the lowered requirement. That will be a loss to society as a whole.

Instead of lowering the admission requirement for some students, the medical school should maintain its standards and add other selection criteria. For all the students whose SAT score is 1,400 and over, they have achieved the minimum standard. The medical school should only accept students from that pool. The medical school can consider other selection criteria but should not reduce the academic requirement to less than a 1,400 SAT score.

A Points System

It is crucial to have a fair system to assess the application of education, employment or social welfare. Fairness can only be based on objective judgements. When applying for a job, we must provide our name and contact information. Some employers even ask for links to view the profiles on social media. From the name, people may be able to tell our ethnicity. Even though it is a typical Western name, people can still find out more personal information by referring to social media or checking the address, telephone number, and schools attended, needless to say, the photos on social media. Therefore, all that information should be hidden before assessing the candidates so that the decision-makers cannot tell the ethnicity, religion and other backgrounds of the candidates to make a fair decision.

Each applicant should be assigned a number as their identification. If there is a need for an interview, an audio conference is better than an online meeting or in-person interview. In an audio conference, the interviewer cannot tell the colour, age, gender orientation and other personal backgrounds of the applicants. The interviewers only know the number assigned and the applicant's rating from the assessment. If needed, the voice of the applicant can also be processed so that it will become a gender-neutral tone so that the interviewers cannot tell if the applicant is a male or female. That way, the decisions can be made objectively without prejudice and discrimination.

Example 1

An American university has a minimum admission requirement of 1,400 SAT scores for its computer engineering department, which is unannounced. They can accept a maximum of 100 students, and there are 2,000 students applied. Of the 2,000 students, 130 applicants have SAT scores below 1,400, and two have the highest score of 1,600.

The 130 applicants with less than 1,400 SAT scores will be disqualified. All other 1,870 applicants will be assessed by their background and be awarded merit points. All applicants are required to fill out an online survey to tell their background so that the university can gather their information for assessment purposes. The table below shows its rating criteria according to the applicants' backgrounds.

Table 2

Status	Points
SAT 1,500 to 1,549	100
SAT 1,550 to 1,599	25
SAT 1,600	100
Indigenous People	100
Black People	25
Other Visible Minorities	10
Female	10
Matured Student (Age 25 and above)	5
Person with Disabilities	20
Overseas Education (per year)	3
LGBT Group	15
Single Parent	10
Veteran	20
Transgendered	50
Fluent in foreign languages (per language)	5
Volunteering (per year, per organization)	2

Each applicant will be assigned a unique application number and rated according to the above criteria. Their acceptance will be solely based on their total scores, with proof of status, identification or achievements as the final admission requirement.

In real life, universities in different countries and cities may need to set up their systems using different criteria and award different points according to their situations, such as demographics and competitions. Some American universities temporarily tried not to require SAT scores as one of their admission requirements. [280] In fact, many universities in the world use local high school grades, International Baccalaureate (IB) scores or the public examination results in their countries to assess the student's academic standards. (Note: The above table is for illustration purposes only.)

<u>Example 2</u>

A conglomerate has several subsidiaries, including manufacturing firms, transportation companies and retail chains. It wants to set standard hiring criteria to recruit people. Each position has a minimum academic requirement plus some years of experience in that field, except for some junior positions. Now, it wants to hire a Senior Accounting Manager for one of its retail chains.

The minimum requirements for the position are a professional accounting designation, ten years of experience in the accounting field, and five years of experience in the managerial grade. Based on those requirements, all applicants without a professional accounting designation, less than ten years of accounting experience and less than five years of managerial experience will be rejected. All applicants are required to fill out an online survey to tell their background

---

[280] "Harvard, Yale and 5 other Ivy League schools will not require SATs or ACTs for admissions next year", CNBC, last updated June 18, 2020, https://www.cnbc.com/2020/06/17/7-ivy-league-schools-will-not-require-sats-or-acts-next-year.html

so that the corporation can gather their information for assessment purposes. The corporation uses the table below to rate the applicants according to their backgrounds.

Table 3

Status	Points
A University Degree	10
A Postgraduate Degree	15
Degree in Accountancy or Finance	5
Experience (for every year over ten years)	1
Managerial Experience (each year over 5 years)	1
Newcomers	100
Ethnic Minorities	5
Female	3
Person with Disabilities	5
Overseas Education (per year)	1
LGBT Group	5
Single Parent	3
Veteran	10
Fluent in foreign languages (per language)	2
Volunteering (per year, per organization)	1
Working Experience with Listed Companies	5
Working Experience with Retail Companies	5

From its criteria, we can tell that an applicant who fulfills the minimum requirements and a newcomer (such as from Mainland China) would probably get the highest scores. The reason is that the corporation assigns 100 points to newcomers, which is significantly higher than the sum of the points that all other categories can get. It is because the corporation wants to give newcomers the absolute advantage once they are qualified for the minimum requirements.

On the other hand, the corporation must constantly review its employees' ethnic distribution and other demographics to ensure true equity. If there is a high percentage of newcomers in the senior manager grade, it may have to lower the points assigned to newcomers in the subsequent recruitment. Otherwise, the points system is not fair to other people. For example, if 2% of the population are newcomers in Hong Kong, but 20% of the managers in the corporation are newcomers, then the points assigned to newcomers should be reduced to a reasonable level.

Example 3

A nonprofit organization focusing on mentoring young people needs to form an advisory group for one of its initiatives. Its minimum requirements are a university degree in any discipline, at least ten years of experience in nonprofit organizations, with at least five years in full-time positions. All applicants without the minimum qualifications will not be considered.

The organization uses the following table to assess the applicants to ensure the advisory group has the broadest diversity. All applicants are required to fill out an online survey to tell their background so that the organization can gather their information for assessment purposes.

Table 4

Age	30 or below	31 to 40	41 to 50	51 to 60	61 to 70	Over 71
Ancestry	African	Asian	European	Hispanic	Indigenous	Muslim
Career	Education	Executive	Nonprofit	General	Government	Technical
Skin Colour	White	Pale	Light Brown	Brown	Black	
Creed	Buddhism	Christian	Judaism	Islam	Hinduism	Other
Citizenship	China	Foreign				
Criminal Record	Yes	No	Pardoned			
Education Level	Elementary	High School	College	University	Post-graduate	Post-doctoral
Education Specialty	Arts	Business	Engineering	Medical	Science	Social Science
Family Status	No Kid	One Kid	Two Kids	Three or more kids		
Gender Identity	Male	Female	Transgender	Intersex		
Language Speak	Indo-European	Sino-Tibetan	Niger-Congo	Afroasiatic	Austronesian	Other
Marital Status	Single	Married	Divorced	Widowed	Cohabitation	Other
Military Experience	None	Less than two years	Less than five years	Less than ten years	Less than twenty years	More than twenty years
Overseas Experience	None	Less than two years	Less than five years	Less than ten years	Less than twenty years	More than twenty years
Physical Disability	No	Visual	Audio	Limbs		
Political Beliefs	A	B	C	D	E	Other
Sexual Orientation	Gay	Lesbian	Bisexual	Other		
Net Worth	Less than $10,000	$10,000 to $100,000	$100,001 to $500,000	$500,001 to $2,500,000	$2,500,001 to $10M	More than $10M

The table shows the possible diversity of the advisors, and the organization wants to fill up as many categories as possible. After one advisor has been appointed, the table should be checked and updated. Although the ideal case is that the selected advisors would cover all the fields in the table, it is possible that some categories are not filled.

Applicants can get one point from the table according to their background if that particular field is not checked (no appointed advisor has the same background as the applicants). That is, each unchecked field is worth one point, and the applicant with the highest points will get the appointment.

Real-Life Situation

The three cases above are just simple examples of how organizations and governments can use a points system to achieve diversity and equity. The categories used in the table will be added or eliminated according to the actual situations, and the points assigned to each status should also be adjusted accordingly. Below are the basic principles for setting such a points system:

1. It must be set according to the local demographic data
2. If there are minimum requirements, such requirements should not be changed for different people
3. The points system must be regularly reviewed and adjusted according to the current situation of the organization
4. Decision-making should be solely based on the points
5. Selection criteria when the applicants have identical scores

6. No in-person or video meeting should be used to avoid the leak of personal information

For #1, both the national and regional demographics should be considered in setting the points. Suppose the national population of visible minorities is 1% of the total, but the regional population of visible minorities is 10%. In that case, the organization in that region should use 10% as the base to set the ratio for visible minorities.

For #2, we should not sacrifice the minimum requirements to give advantages to any group of people. If such minimum requirements can be changed, they should be adjusted for all applicants or candidates.

For #3, organizations should review their points system regularly to avoid giving too many preferential treatments to specific groups of people. For example, 50% of the employees of a corporation are visible minorities, while the national population and regional population of visible minorities are only 10% and 20%, respectively. The corporation may have to stop giving merit points to visible minorities until the following review.

For#4, all personal information about the applicants or candidates, including names and addresses, should be hidden from the decision-makers. That is the only way to ensure that decision-makers will not have any personal preference, prejudice, or discrimination against any of them.

Only their total points and application numbers assigned are to be known to the decision-makers.

For#5, it is possible that there are top applicants with identical scores, and the number of people is more than the number of vacancies available. In such a case, the organization may have preset selection criteria for further screening. For example, Indigenous people may always get the advantage in that case, or an LGBT group member will get it. However, the criteria should be a long list to avoid a dead end. What if there are more Indigenous or LGBT group members than required, or there is no Indigenous or LGBT group member on the top list?

For #6, instead of having the selection criteria in #5, the decision-makers may arrange interviews for the applicants with identical top scores. As discussed in the sections above, such interviews should avoid the leak of personal information about the applications, mainly their race and skin colour. Therefore, an audio conference instead of a video meeting or in-person interview should be used so that the decision-makers cannot tell the background of the applicants from the interview.

The points system ensures that resources are fairly distributed, and people are served or recruited fairly and diversely. It can also give preferential benefits to disadvantaged groups. The importance of the process is to maintain its objective measure. Personal information, such as race, age and gender, must be gathered to fairly evaluate them and give some applicants preferential treatment as positive discrimination. However, we must protect their privacy so that their personal information should not be known to the decision-makers to avoid any preference, prejudice, or discrimination.

To conclude, diversity can be done by objectively assessing the people involved, which computer programs can do. However, inclusion must be done by people. Therefore, educating people to accept differences, such as cultures, beliefs, and races, is paramount.

An Example in Hong Kong

Suppose AAA Limited, a retail chain specializing in cosmetics products, is looking for a district manager to oversee their retail outlets in the Greater Bay Area. The company hires around 250 employees with headquarters in Hong Kong. The management wants to expand the market in mainland China. They want to recruit an experienced retail manager within their industry. They post the following requirements on their advertisements:

- A bachelor's degree, business-related preferred
- Fluent Cantonese and Putonghua
- At least five years of retail management experience
- Experience in the cosmetics industry is preferred
- Strong customer service and interpersonal skills
- A team leader able to influence peers

- A proactive self-starter
- A problem solver
- Strong negotiation and communication skills
- Collaborative style with internal and external customers
- Competency in computer usage

To help the management recruit the district manager using a diversified approach, we first have to classify their requirements into "must-have" and "nice to have" two categories. We created a table to separate the requirements as below:

Table 5

Must-have	Nice to have
A bachelor's degree	Degree in a business subject
Five years of retail management experience	More than five years of retail management experience
Customer service and interpersonal skills	Experience in the cosmetics industry
A team leader	Collaborative style
A proactive self-starter	Competency in computer usage
Negotiation and communication skills	A problem solver
Fluent in Cantonese and Putonghua	

These two types of requirements can be further divided into two sub-categories - binary options and multiple options. Binary options have the answer Yes or No. Multiple options typically link with the quantity, such as the number of years or ratings. We have the tables below:

Table 6

Must-have	
Binary Options	**Multiple Options**
A bachelor's degree	Customer service and interpersonal skills
Five years of retail management experience	Negotiation and communication skills
Fluent in Cantonese and Putonghua	Proactive self-starter
	A team leader

Table 7

Nice to have	
Binary Options	**Multiple Options**
Degree in a business-related subject	More than five years of retail management experience
	Experience in the cosmetics industry
	Collaborative style
	Competency in computer usage
	A problem solver

Since the binary must-have options are mandatory, candidates will only be considered if they possess those characteristics. Therefore, they have only two options – have no point or a fixed point. Multiple must-have options can have more than two options – no point or different levels of points. A points system based on these basic requirements is created as below. A candidate who scores a zero in any category in the table will not be considered.

Table 8

Must-have		
A candidate who scores a Zero in any category below will not be considered.		
Requirement	Points Assign	Points Scored
A bachelor's degree	0 for No 10 for Yes	
Five years of retail management experience	0 for less than five years 10 for five years or more	
Fluent in Cantonese and Putonghua	0 for No 10 for Yes	
Customer service and interpersonal skills*	0 to 3	
A team leader*	0 to 3	
A proactive self-starter*	0 to 3	
Negotiation and communication skills*	0 to 3	
* Based on the candidate's background and interview performance.		

The rating of "Customer service and interpersonal skills", "A team leader", "A proactive self-starter", and "Negotiation and communication skills" are very subjective. The interviewers should never rate a candidate zero unless they have negative feelings about the performance of the candidate in that category during the interview or are confident that the candidate has no such skills. The minimum and maximum points a qualified candidate can earn from the must-have categories are 34 and 42, respectively.

Similarly, a table for the nice-to-have categories is created below.

Table 9

Nice-to-have		
Requirement	Points Assign	Points Scored
Degree in a business-related subject	0 for No 5 for Yes	
More than five years of retail management experience	1 for each year exceeds 5 yrs (max 5 points)	
Experience in the cosmetics industry	1 for each year (max 5 points)	
Collaborative style*	0 or 1	
Competency in computer usage*	0 or 1	
A problem solver*	0 or 1	
* Based on the candidate's background and interview performance.		

The maximum number of points a qualified candidate can earn from the nice-to-have categories is 18, making the maximum number of points a qualified candidate can earn from both streams 60. Except for "International experience", there is no point assigned for diversification purposes. Before creating a points system for diversification purposes, we must study the demographics of Hong Kong (Table 1) and China.[281]

To support newcomers to Hong Kong, the company assigns 30 points to the applicants who immigrated to Hong Kong in the last ten years. Han is the majority ethnic group in Hong Kong and the Mainland, and coincidentally, both are 92% of their populations. Currently, AAA Limited does not have any employees who are minorities. Therefore, the management decided to assign a heavy score of 30 points to minorities. That will boost minority groups from a minimum score of 34 from the combined Must-have and Nice-to-have categories to the minimum score of 64 so that they can compete with others with advantages.

Although 54.3% of the Hong Kong population are women, females have historical disadvantages and need a boost, especially at the management level of a corporation. Moreover, only 32% of AAA Limited's middle and senior managers are female. Therefore, the management decided to assign 10 points to them. They also assign a maximum of 10

---

[281] "Demographics of China", Wikipedia, last accessed September 23, 2023, https://en.wikipedia.org/wiki/Demographics_of_China

points to those who have overseas working experience or have studied overseas.

For other disadvantaged groups, 15 points are assigned to persons with disabilities, 10 points to the LGBT group, and single parents will also get 5 points. People who are fluent in other languages (including English) can earn 3 points for each language. Each year of experience in volunteering also receives 1 point. Age is not a factor to be considered in this case as it is included in the "experience" category. We have the table below:

Table 10

Other Factors		
Requirement	Points Assign	Points Scored
Newcomer	30	
Minority groups	30	
Female	10	
Overseas experience	1 per year, max 10	
Person with Disabilities	15	
LGBT group	10	
Single parent	5	
Fluent in other languages (per language)	3 each	
Volunteering (per year, per organization)	5 max	

The following table is formed after combining the three tables above:

Table 11

Requirement	Points Assign	Score
Must-have Categories		
A bachelor's degree	0 for No 10 for Yes	
Five years of retail management experience	0 for less than 5 years 10 for 5 years or more	
Fluent in Cantonese and Putonghua	0 for No 10 for Yes	
Customer service and interpersonal skills*	0 to 3	
A team leader*	0 to 3	
A proactive self-starter*	0 to 3	
Negotiation and communication skills*	0 to 3	
Nice-to-have Categories		
Degree in a business-related subject	0 for No 5 for Yes	
More than five years of retail management experience	1 for each year exceeds 5 years (max 5 points)	
Experience in the cosmetics industry	1 for each year (max 5 points)	
Collaborative style*	0 or 1	
Competency in computer usage*	0 or 1	
A problem solver*	0 or 1	
Degree in a business-related subject	0 for No 5 for Yes	
Other Categories		
Newcomer	30	
Minority groups	30	
Female	10	
Overseas experience	1 per year, max 10	
Person with Disabilities	15	

LGBT group	10	
Single parent	5	
Fluent in other languages (per language)	3 each	
Volunteering (per year, per organization)	5 max	
TOTAL		
* Based on the candidate's background and interview performance.		

Conclusion

Diversity is based on the demographics of the local populations and expanded to other disadvantaged groups according to society's needs. Diversity cannot sacrifice the minimum standards or requirements of the selection process. A points system for hiring an executive is not the same as hiring junior staff, and the demographics of a large organization are constantly changing. Therefore, the points system must be regularly reviewed and adjusted according to the case and the current demographics of the organization and the local municipality or region.

The points assigned to each category are unavoidably subjective, but they should be reasonable. The table should be set according to the organization's existing structure, agreed by the management, and be able to withstand any challenge. The management can add more categories to the table as long as those are human characteristics and non-discriminative.

Inclusion is a culture that an organization must set up, promote and maintain. Inclusion is about people's right to participate and the organization's duty to accept them. Accepting them includes providing them with a stressless and comfortable environment without the fear of discrimination. Empathy is the crucial key to achieving inclusion.

Equity will finally be reached with a well-structured, diversified selection process and an inclusive environment. The concept of equity, diversity and inclusion is not a matter of political correctness; it is the key for everyone to succeed.

Appendix. Glossary

Ableism: discrimination and social prejudice against people with disabilities or who are perceived to have disabilities. Ableism can be conscious or unconscious and is embedded in communities, institutions, systems, or society's broader culture.

Aboriginal Peoples: See Indigenous Peoples

Accessibility: a general term for the degree of ease that something (e.g., building, device, service, and information) can be accessed, used and enjoyed by persons with disabilities. Easy accessibility benefits the general population, such as seniors and families with small children, by making things more usable and practical for everyone.

Accessible: does not have obstacles for people with disabilities — something that can be easily reached or obtained; facilities that can be easily entered; information that is easy to retrieve.

Adaptive Technologies: the technologies used in some products to help people with vision, hearing, mobility or other disabilities to use the products.

Adverse Impact: having a harmful result. Treating people with and without disabilities the same will have a negative effect on some people.

Affirmative Action: action designed to address the historical disadvantage that identifiable groups (e.g., women and visible minorities) have experienced by increasing their representation in employment, higher education or treatment.

African Canadian: a Canadian of African origin or descent.

Ageism: stereotyping against individuals or groups based on their age, generally with discrimination.

Ally: a member of the dominant group who is against oppression.

Alternative (Alternate) Format: a method of communication that considers the disability of a person, such as an audiobook instead of a print version for someone with a visual disability.

Anti-racism (Anti-oppression): an active and consistent process of change to eliminate racism and the oppression and injustice racism causes.

Assistive device: devices to help people, primarily people with disabilities, perform a task, such as an assistive listening device, forklift and wheelchair.

Audism: a belief that a person is superior or inferior based on their ability to hear or act like a person who hears.

Barrier: anything that prevents a person from fully taking part in all aspects of society, including physical, information or communications, attitudinal, economic and technological barriers, as well as policies or practices.

BFOR: acronym for Bona Fide Occupational Requirement, a defence used in discrimination in employment.

Bias: a predisposition, prejudice or generalization about a group of persons based on characteristics or stereotypes.

Bigotry: obstinate or unreasonable attachment to a belief, opinion, or prejudice against a person or people based on stereotypes related to age, race, religion, sexual orientation, and more.

Biological Sex: the biological classification of people as male or female. A doctor assigns sex at birth by visually assessing external anatomy. Sex terms are "male", "female", and "intersex".

Biracial: a person whose ancestry includes members of two racial groups.

Bisexual: a person who is emotionally, physically, sexually or spiritually attracted to members of more than one gender.

Black: a social construct referring to people who have dark skin colour or other related racialized characteristics. Diverse societies apply different criteria to determine who is Black.

Caste System: a form of social stratification with roots in India's ancient history and persisting to the present time. This system divides its people into four different classes: Brahmin, Kshatriya, Vaishya, and Shudra. In addition to the four major castes, another type of people called Dalit or untouchable is excluded from the castes.

Caucasian: an outdated term that often has been used as a synonym for white.

Characteristics: a personal trait or attribute.

Civil Union: a legally recognized arrangement similar to a marriage, created primarily as a means to provide recognition in law for same-sex couples.

Code: refers to the human rights code of the local jurisdiction.

Coming Out: the often life-long process of discovering, defining and proclaiming one's sexuality (usually non-heterosexual).

Competing Rights: situations where parties to a dispute claim that the enjoyment of an individual or group's human rights and freedoms, as protected by law, would interfere with another's rights and freedoms.

Culture: the achievements, behaviours, beliefs or customs of a particular time or people; behaviour within a particular group.

Cultural Competence: an ability to interact effectively with people of different cultural or ethnic backgrounds.

Culturally Competent Organization: an organization that displays cultural competence, in both its systems and individual behaviour.

Custom: a traditional practice.

DDO: Disability Discrimination Ordinance (Cap. 487)

Dimensions of Diversity: the unique personal characteristics that distinguish people as individuals and groups. These include, but are not limited to, age, gender, race, sex, ethnicity, physical and intellectual ability, class, creed, religion and sexual orientation.

Disability: it covers a broad range and degree of conditions, some visible and some not visible. A disability may have been present from birth, caused by accident, or developed over time. There are physical, mental, cognitive and learning disabilities, mental disorders, hearing or vision disabilities, epilepsy, drug and alcohol dependencies, environmental sensitivities, and other conditions.

Discrimination: treating someone unfairly by either imposing a burden on them or denying them a benefit, privilege or opportunity enjoyed by others because of their characteristics such as age, religion, family status, disability, sex and race.

Duty to Accommodate: people identified by human rights law are entitled to the same opportunities and benefits as everybody else.

East Asian People: people who share ancestry, heritage and culture from several countries and regions, including China, Hong Kong, Japan, Macau, Mongolia, North Korea, South Korea, Taiwan and Vietnam.

EDI: abbreviation of Equity, Diversity and Inclusion.

Elder: a distinguished man or woman recognized in the Aboriginal community for the gift of healing, spiritual or wisdom leadership.

EOC: the acronym for Equal Opportunities Commission of Hong Kong

Equal Opportunity: to ensure that all people have equal access, free of barriers, equal participation and equal benefit from whatever an organization offers.

Equal Treatment: treatment that brings about equality of access, such as providing a ramp for wheelchair access to a building in addition to a stair.

Equitable: just or characterized by fairness or equity.

Equity: the quality of fairness, impartiality, even-handedness.

Ethnicity: sharing a distinctive cultural and historical tradition associated with ancestry, creed, place of origin or race.

Exclusion: denying or limiting access to a place, group, privilege, and more.

FDO: Family Status Discrimination Ordinance (Cap. 527)

Francophone: people who have advanced knowledge of French and use it at home, including people whose mother tongue may not be French.

Gay: persons who have an emotional, physical, sexual or spiritual attraction to persons of the same sex.

Gender: the social classification of people as masculine or feminine.

Gender Identity: the conscious sense of maleness or femaleness of a person. This sense of self is separate and distinct from one's biological sex.

Harassment: engaging in the course of comments or actions known (or ought reasonably to be known) to be unwelcome. It can involve words or actions known (or ought reasonably to be known) to be demeaning, embarrassing, humiliating, offensive, or unwelcome.

Hate Activity: negative comments or unfriendly actions against a person or group motivated by bias, prejudice or hate based on, including but not limited to: age, ancestry, race, ethnic origin, language, colour, religion, mental disability, physical disability, family status, marital status, sex, sexual orientation.

Heightism: prejudice or discrimination against individuals based on height.

Heterosexual: persons who have an emotional, physical, sexual or spiritual attraction to persons of the opposite sex.

Heterosexism: a belief that heterosexuality is superior and preferable to other sexualities and that heterosexuality is the only right, normal or moral expression of sexuality.

Historical Disadvantage: a disadvantage that results from historical patterns of institutionalized and other forms of systemic discrimination.

Homosexual: an outdated term for persons with an emotional, physical, sexual or spiritual attraction to persons of the same sex. It is more of a medical term and may insult lesbian and gay people or the LGBT community.

Homophobia: the irrational aversion to, fear or hatred of people who are identified or perceived as being lesbian, gay, bisexual or transgender (LGBT).

Impairment: a physical, sensory, intellectual, learning or medical condition, including mental illness, that limits functioning or requires accommodation.

Inclusion: appreciating and using our unique differences – strengths, talents, weaknesses and frailties – in a way that shows respect for the individual and ultimately creates a dynamic multi-dimensional community.

Inclusive Design: taking differences among individuals and groups into consideration when designing something to avoid creating barriers. Inclusive design can apply to systems, facilities, programs, policies, services, education, and more.

Indigenous Peoples: a collective name for the native people who inhabited a country or a geographical region at the time when people of different cultures or ethnic origins arrived.

Intellectual Disability: also called a developmental disability, involves significant limitations both in intellectual functioning (reasoning, learning, problem-solving) and in adaptive behaviour, which covers a range of everyday social and practical skills.

Intergenerational: existing or occurring between different generations of people, involving more than one generation.

Intersex: a term used for a variety of conditions in which a person is born with a genital that does not seem to fit the typical definitions of female or male, formerly inappropriately referred to as hermaphrodites. Most intersex people do not possess "both" sets of genitals but rather a blending or a different appearance that is medically difficult to categorize for many doctors.

Lesbian: a woman who has an emotional, physical, sexual or spiritual attraction to other women.

LGBT: an acronym for Lesbian, Gay, Bisexual and Transgender. Sometimes, GLBT is also used.

LGBTTIQQ2A: an acronym for Lesbian, Gay, Bisexual, Transgender, Transsexual, Intersex, Queer, Questioning, 2-spirited and Allies.

Merit: picking a candidate for a position who meets job-related selection criteria, such as experience, knowledge and skills, at the level required for a position or assignment.

MSM: an abbreviation of Men who have Sex with Men.

Multiracial: a person whose heritage includes members of multiple racial groups.

Native Groups: Indigenous people in the United States.

Newcomers: New immigrants in countries of immigration, such as Australia, Canada and the United States.

Pay Equity: the principle of equal pay for work of equal value. For example, the principle is applied to pay male and female employees within the same organization the same salary for work that is judged to be of equal value.

Persons of Colour: an inclusive term encompassing a range of social identity groups based on their skin colour, such as Asians, Aboriginal Peoples, Hispanics and Blacks.

Persons with Disabilities: persons with one or more long-term or recurring disabilities.

Poisoned Work Environment: a negative, hostile or unpleasant workplace due to comments or conduct that tend to demean a group identified by one or more prohibited grounds under any Human Rights Act or Code, even if not directed at a specific individual.

Power: access to privileges such as connections, decision-making, experience, expertise, resources, knowledge and information, enhancing a person's chances of getting what they need to live a comfortable, safe, productive and profitable life.

Prejudice: affective feeling or negative prejudgment about another person or group of persons based on perceived characteristics.

Pride: a term used about the LGBT community. It means people not being ashamed of themselves or showing their pride to others by "coming out", marching in the Pride parade or similar parades, and being honest and comfortable about who they are.

Pride Parade: an outdoor event that celebrates LGBT achievements, legal rights, pride, self and social acceptance

Privilege: unearned access, advantages, benefits, opportunities or power that exist for members of the dominant groups in society. It can also refer to the relative privilege of one group compared to another.

Prohibited Grounds (Protected Grounds): the personal characteristics that the human rights law based on to prohibit discrimination or harassment. The common protected grounds include age, ancestry, citizenship, colour, creed, disability, ethnic origin, family status, gender identity and gender expression, marital status, place of origin, race, receipt of public assistance (in housing), a record of offences (in employment), sex and sexual orientation.

Queer: formerly derogatory slang term used to identify sexual and gender minorities who are not heterosexual.

Questioning: exploring one's own sexual or gender identity, looking at such things as upbringing, expectations from others, such as friends and employers, and inner motivation.

Race: a group of people with similar geographic, historical, political, economic, physical, social, and cultural factors.

Racialization: the process by which societies construct races as real, different and unequal in ways that matter and affect economic, political and social life.

Racial Profiling: any action that relies on stereotypes about race, ancestry, colour, ethnicity, religion or place of origin, or a combination of these, rather than on a reasonable suspicion to single out a person for greater scrutiny or different treatment.

Racism: a belief that one race group is superior or inferior to others.

RDO: Race Discrimination Ordinance (Cap. 602)

SDO: Sex Discrimination Ordinance (Cap. 480)

Sexism: a belief that one gender type is superior or inferior to another, usually linked with discrimination.

Sexual Orientation: the direction of one's sexual interest or attraction. It covers the range of human sexuality from lesbian and gay to bisexual and heterosexual.

South Asian: a native or inhabitant of the Indian subcontinent, including Afghanistan, Bangladesh, Bhutan, India, the Maldives, Nepal, Pakistan, and Sri Lanka.

Status Indian: a person recognized by the federal government as being registered under the *Indian Act*, also referred to as a Registered Indian.

Stereotype: incorrect assumption based on age, sex, race, colour, ethnic origin, religion, and more. Stereotyping typically involves attributing the same characteristics to all members of a group regardless of their differences.

Straight: an informal term for Heterosexual.

Systemic Barrier: a barrier embedded in the administrative or social structures of an organization, including the culture of an organization, decision-making processes, the physical accessibility of an organization, and organizational policies and practices. The barrier may exclude members of groups protected by human rights law.

Systemic Discrimination: patterns of behaviour, policies or practices that are part of the social or administrative structures of an organization and which create or perpetuate a position of relative disadvantage for groups identified under the human rights law.

Two-Spirit: a term that refers to Aboriginal people who are gay, lesbian, bisexual, or trans-gendered.

Transgender (or Trans): a person whose biological sex assigned at birth does not match their gender identity.

Transsexual: persons who are identified at birth as one sex but who identify themselves differently and have undergone one or more medical treatments to align their bodies with their internally felt identity. While some people embrace this term as an identity, it is rejected by others.

West Indian: a person from the West Indies, including Antigua and Barbuda, Bahamas, Barbados, Cuba, Dominica, Dominican Republic, Grenada, Haiti, Jamaica, Saint Kitts and Nevis, Saint Lucia, Saint Vincent and the Grenadines, Trinidad and Tobago.

White: people belonging to any of various peoples with light-coloured skin, usually of European origin. The term has become an indicator less of skin colour and more of racialized characteristics.

www.ingramcontent.com/pod-product-compliance
Lightning Source LLC
Chambersburg PA
CBHW061253220326
41599CB00028B/5640